THE PRACTICAL ENCYCLOPEDIA OF

Good Decorating
and Home Improvement

THE PRACTICAL ENCYCLOPEDIA OF

Good Decorating

and Home Improvement

GREYSTONE PRESS

About Your Encyclopedia

Here, at your fingertips, is the most comprehensive and complete encyclopedia on home decorating and improvement ever assembled. In these pages, you will discover how to make your home more beautiful, more comfortable, and more livable—all at the lowest possible cost.

Whether you plan to add on an extra bedroom, expand a kitchen, build a new patio, decorate the living room, den or what have

you—your encyclopedia can save you thousands of dollars. And with today's rising and inflated costs in both labor and materials, your encyclopedia takes on an even greater importance.

Recent studies show that in the furniture and appliance industry alone, items for the home were produced at a retail value of more than *nine billion dollars;* in the home improvement industry, the value was *twelve to fourteen billion dollars*. And these figures don't include such items as fabrics, pictures, accessories, mattresses and springs, bedding and linens, china, silver, glassware, or lighting. As you can imagine, many purchasers spent too much for too little. And more often than not, it was simply because they weren't sure of what they were buying or how to make the right selection at the lowest price.

This is where your encyclopedia is a necessity. It shows you how to save money in every area of home decorating and improvement. From the first entry right through to the last, this encyclopedia tells you hundreds of ways you can cut costs and how you can buy wisely.

Over 60 expert interior designers, artists, architects, writers, and photographers spent many years developing material for this important encyclopedia. More than 4,000 photographs are used to show you the basics of good decorating and the how-to of home improvement. Easy to understand, easy to follow, your encyclopedia offers step-by-step instructions on how to create the home of your dreams. Here's how to use color, what window arrangements to use, where to add on that extra room, how to save money picking one fabric over another and literally dozens of budget ideas.

Of course, your encyclopedia is more than just a money-saver. If you don't already know, you'll soon discover that few things in life are more satisfying or rewarding than decorating or remodeling your own home. Here you have the work and ideas of famous interior designers and architects on which you can draw to help you create a home that is distinctively and uniquely your own. Your encyclopedia is designed to help guide *you* in developing good taste and discrimination, to build confidence in your judgment, to let your imagination have free rein, and most important—to let you express your individuality in and through your home.

Briefly then, it is designed for your convenient and immediate use. You have in your hands a *complete* decorating and home improvement encyclopedia that can help you make your home not only beautiful, comfortable, and livable—but also a happy home.

The Editors

Contributors

Editorial Consultants

KARL L. STEINHAUSER, AID, NSID, Chicago
Design consultant to furnishings manufacturers
Magazine Decorating Editor for 8 years

A. ALLEN DIZIK, FAID, Los Angeles
Board of Governors, Am. Inst. of Interior Design
Inaugurated, published AID Magazine

PATRICIA HARVEY, AID, New York City
Advisory Board, National Design Center
Former Board Member, NSID

EDMUND T. LAWYER, AID, Philadelphia
Design consultant for home fashions and advertising
A former Decorating Editor

PAUL KRAUSS, New York City
Noted Interior Designer of residences, offices, bldgs.
Creator of environmental images for industry

PETER K. RYAN, Windsor, Ontario, Canada
Heads Canadian Interior Design firm
Corp. Member, AID, Interior Designers of Ontario

Designers and Decorators

Douglas Allison
Ethyl Alper, AID
Rose Aronin, NSID
Don Bailey, AID
Lee Bailey
David Barrett
Sidney Blackard
Lee Blake
David Blumenthal
Ann Bolitski
Milton A. Botterill, AID
Roger Bracy, AID
Jack Brandt Ltd.
Rhonda Bright, AID
Everett Brown, FAID
Yale R. Burge, NSID
Arthur Burke
William Busam, AID
Stephen Chase
Rosanne Clark
George Cody
Joseph Copp, Jr.
Meanette Coppes, NSID
James Corbett
Luis Cordano, AID
Jini Costello, AID

Marvin Culbreth, AID, NSID
William Denler, AID
George Doan, AID
Angelo Donghia
Allyn Dunkin
Mrs. Yardley Elder, AID
John Elmo, AID
Arthur Elrod, AID
James Fisher
Carla Flood, AID
Lenore Friedman, NSID
Keith Gasser
Dorian Grant
Ed San Gregori
Les Grodsky
Kenneth Harder
Al Herbert
Richard Himmel
Harold Holtz
Jinney Lee Show
Jon-Thomas, Inc.
Ione Keenan, NSID
Roy Klipp, AID
Corrine Krisel
Martin Kuckly
William Lanyon

Evelyn Leroy, NSID
Robert Lindenthal, NSID
Lisbon Interiors
J. Frederick Lohman, AID
John Lombardi
Betty Lotz, AID
James Lumsden
Tom Mallory
Shirley Marks, NSID
William E. Mathers, AID
Ellen McClusky, FAID
William McNutt, AID
Robert Melin
Lee Merban Assoc.
Kitty Mercer, AID
Howard Miller
Warren Moen
James Childs Morse, AID
Edmund Motyka, AID
Harry Nardi
Mark Nelson
Bernard Nusinow, AID
Davis Parry
Dorothy Paul, AID
Lawrence Peabody
Albert Pensis, AID
James E. Peterson, AID
Alan Patt, NSID
Raymond Piatti
Barbara Pinsof

Joseph Potter, AID
Audrey Price
Mabel Rea
Shirley Regendahl
L. Jarmon Roach, AID
Helen Rosenthal
Lynn Rotblatt, NSID
Gertrude Ruben, AID
Ethel Samuels, NSID
Agatha Schoenbrun, AID
Neil Van Sciver
Severs & van Engen
Gerald Siegwart
Leroy Small
Ving and Charlotte Smith
Morley B. Smith
Lewis Solloway
Rita St. Clair
C. E. Stephenson, AID
J. Neil Stevens, NSID
Myrtle Todes
Gerald Tomlin, AID
Donald Weber, AID
Sally Welch
Herbert Wells
Sandy White
Ceil Williams, AID, NSID
Randall Williams
Don Williams
Tom Woods, AID

Architects

Irving M. Addis	Harry Bates
Stanley Anderson Assoc.	William Bernondy, AID
J. Donald Bowman	F. Frederick Bruck
Joel Brand	Robert A. Burley
Wayne R. Nordgren	Richard W. Searcy
Franklin Paul	Isadore Shank, AIA
Olga Paul	Kenneth Triester, AIA
Harry Ranson	Norman Ufer
Don Reiman, AIA	Lester Wertheimer, AIA
George B. Roberts	Jon Winkelstein, AIA
Harold Buttrick	Karl Humphrey
Frank W. Cauley	J. William Ilmanen
Edward Diehl Associates	Raymond F. Johnson
Edward H. Fickett, AIA	William Krisel, AIA
John L. Field	Richard H. Kruse
Knox Griffin	Ernest Mandel

Artists and Photographers

Horst Ahlberg	Mike Dieter
Edward A. Bourdon	Hedrich-Blessing
Frank Davis	Herrlin
de Gennaro	Carlos Diniz Associates
Bill Hopkins	Warren Reynolds
Lisanti	Rogers
Obata Studios	Stanley Warren
Pearson	Dick Larson

Museums, Institutes, and Others

Cabin Crafts	Edward Fields
Amtico	Illinois Shade Div.,
Bigelow-Sanford, Inc.	Slick Industrial Co.
American Cyanamid Co.	Stauffer Chemical Co.
Stockwell Wallcoverings	Masonite
Syroco	Institute of High
Eastman Kodel	Fidelity
Celanese Corp.	Royal Systems, Inc.
Allied Chemical Corp.	Myercord Co.
U.S. Rubber Co.	Colony Totine
Mutschler Bros. Co.	Hercules, Inc.
The Art Foundry Div. of	GAF Corporation
Rexall Drug and Chemical	E. I. duPont
Selig	de Nemours & Co., Inc.
Stanley Furn. Co.	Martin Senour Paints
Art Institute of Chicago	American Carpet Institute
Englander	Dorfile Mfg.
Monsanto	The Viking Sauna Co.
Ponderosa Pine	National Cotton Council
Woodwork Assoc.	Tressard
Greeff Fabrics	Stiffel
Breneman, Inc.	Heywood—Wakefield
Columbus Coated Fabrics	Barclay Mfg. Co., Inc.
J. P. Stevens	Beadangles
Tampa Electric	Baumritter
Parkwood Laminates, Inc.	Union Carbide Corp.
Nettle Creek Industries	The Birge Co.
American Standard	Kirsch Corp.
Joanna Western Mills Co.	Latex Foam Institute
Window Shade	Title Council of America
Manufacturers Assoc.	North American Sauna
Fine Hardwoods Assocation	National Design Center

Editorial Staff

Joseph P. King, Executive Editor
Donald J. Dooley, Editorial Director
Malcolm E. Robinson, Managing Editor
John Berg, Art Director
Marie Schutz, Associate Editor
David Kastler, Associate Editor
Janice McCord, Assistant Editor
Designers: Ron Garman, Arthur Riser, George Meininger,
Contributing Editors: Jo Bull, Kay Stroud, Dorothy Ewing,
Ann Joselyn, Audrey King, Elizabeth Matthews, Barbara Neal,
Jane Staley, Jane Graf Evers, Nancy Textor, Lucille Albrecht,
Helen Schubert, Ruth Wolfson

We have listed only a few of the important contributors who
have helped make your *Practical Encyclopedia of Good
Decorating and Home Improvement* possible. We wish to
give special thanks to Norman Ginsberg and the National
Design Center for their cooperation in releasing more t1an
150 color photographs for use in these volumes.

Highlights and Highpoints

The complete *Practical Encyclopedia of Good Decorating and Home Improvement* answers thousands of questions — solves thousands of decorating and improvement problems. For example, in the first three volumes alone, you will find:

ABC'S of Decorating: how to put your personality into your home or apartment — how to use the color wheel — basic color schemes — effects of light on color—how to prepare your color scheme —how to choose patterns and textures—essentials of room and furniture arrangement — how to select the proper floor treatment — walls — windows and window treatments — fabrics and wall coverings.

Accessories and Accents: how to use objects you love to bring life to your rooms — how to use walls as backgrounds — how to select accents and accessories — how to decorate for height — how to capture a mood — how to banish clutter for - ever — all about shelves and shelving — rugs and where to use them — how to care for area rugs — shopping tips and guidance — how to use floor cushions, pillows and accessories as finishing touches — all about lights and lighting fixtures.

Additions: how to expand your house's usefulness, beauty and size — how to choose a contractor — financing your addition — how to find new uses for old rooms — how to add family rooms, multipurpose rooms, living rooms, office and guest rooms, kitchens, patios, outdoor living areas.

Alcoves: what to do with a niche or recessed area– how to use an alcove as a vanity — how to use old closets for new ideas — how to make use of the very small room — how to find new uses for old hallways — how to create office space at home.

American Styles: how to understand and decorate with Colonial Styles — American Chippendale — Early Federal Period — American Empire and Victorian Style.

Antiques: how to find and use antiques — how to determine authenticity—how to hunt for antique bargains — how to care for antiques — how to decorate with antiques — how to use antiques as accessories — how to determine value.

Antiquing: how to work with wood — the antiquing kit — antique glazes — an easy 4-step method —

how to achieve a splatter pattern—types of wood finishes — waxing and staining.

Apartment Living: ideas to suit your budget and your personality — understanding your apartment lease — what you can and cannot do — planning — how to use color as the pacesetter — style, space and scale — windows and window treatments — floors and tiles — how to get the most light — how to use accessories — arrangements for convenience and beauty—special treatments for kitchens and bathrooms — closets and storage space — budget ideas and projects.

Arches: how to use arches – major structural changes — how to use arched openings to harmonize rooms of related functions — how to enhance your decorating scheme with a blending of curved and straight lines — how to hide unattractive structural features — dramatic uses to highlight decorating schemes.

Architecture: the history of styles—American styles — how to choose the style that fits your needs — uses of wood, siding, aluminum, combinations — how to choose an architect.

Art: painting and sculpture – special lighting for fine art in the home — how to begin a collection without spending a fortune — how to use reproductions — framing — how to use ceramics.

Atmosphere: how to achieve the total effect — how to use color to create mood—how to make rooms look larger and brighter — the elegant materials: velvet, tapestry, brocade and satin — how to balance lighting — how to select a mood.

Atrium: ideas for gardens inside your home—selection of appropriate plants — how to use dwarf and ornamental trees—how to prepare the floors.

Attics: how to turn that half-forgotten room at the top of the stairs into that extra room you have always needed — a playroom — an office — a sewing room — a multi-purpose family room — a guest room — a den — how to work with problem attics — how to solve lighting problems — how to use skylights — how to finish an attic yourself — how to choose and install insulation.

Auctions: choose the right auction for your needs—farm auctions — how to determine what kind of a buyer you want to be — how to bid and buy home furnishings, art objects and antiques.

Avant-Garde: how to use home furnishings that are a step ahead of the times — how to decorate with functional furniture — how to use color as the key element.

Backgrounds: how to use your walls, ceilings, floors and window treatments to set the stage for your entire home—how to use the size, shape and height of rooms to your advantage — how to change the size of rooms with color — how to use draperies to make a small room look larger.

Balance: how to blend height, color and pattern to achieve a well-balanced room — how to plan the room on paper—how to use formal and informal balance for variety.

Barbecues: how to plan for indoor as well as outdoor barbecues—budget barbecues—how to create an outdoor living area.

Basements: how to convert unused basement space into living, working and playing areas — how to tailor your basement to your family needs—how to prepare the basic floor plan — how to plan storage space — how to make stairways safe and attractive.

Baskets: how to use baskets as decorative and functional accents — how to relate the size and shape of baskets to your decorating scheme — how to convert baskets into shades for lights and fixtures — how to use baskets on your patio.

Bathrooms: how to plan for style, comfort and color, whether you are adding a bath or remodeling an old one — three questions to ask yourself before you start — how to find the space you need in the family bath—how to decorate a guest bath — how to add convenience to a children's bath—color schemes for children's bath—how to divide space in your bath — how to prepare a floorplan — how to provide for adequate storage —bathroom lighting—fixtures and fittings—how to remodel your old bath.

Beamed Ceilings: how to add flair, style and color to contemporary or classic homes — how to dress up an old house — how to use beams as a part of your overall decorating plan.

Bedding and Bed Linens: how to choose the right size bed — how to select a matress for maximum comfort — tips and guidance on how to buy a mattress and springs — how to choose pillows.

Bedrooms: how to plan for comfort first — how to stay within your budget — how to decide on what kind of a bedroom you need — how to decorate the master bedroom, children's rooms, guest bedrooms — how to select furniture — how to use pictures to bring rooms to life — how to use accessories as a part of your plan.

Blinds and Shades: how to color-coordinate shades and blinds to give windows a bright new dimension — how to select the right shades for your needs—how to solve special window problems—how to select shade styles—how to adjust shades and blinds.

Bookcases and Bookshelves: how to make them a part of your decorating plan — how to plan and build self-storage units — how to plan for furniture arrangement — how to find wall space for books — how to plan proper lighting for books — how to use books as a center of interest — how to arrange bookshelves—how to team books with accessories — how to get double use from bookcases and book shelves — how to build bookshelves — how to design bookshelves — how to plan for proper fit — how to plan for divider bookcases.

And, the first three volumes are only the beginning — only a tiny fraction of the tips, guidance, advice and inspiration you will get in the complete Encyclopedia. Because of the space limitations in this volume it would be impossible to give you the comprehensive contents of the remaining volumes. But, here is a brief sample:

Budget Ideas: 52 pages of exciting ideas you can execute yourself. **Buffets:** How to plan for serving and how to decorate.

Cabinets: Types, how to choose, and decorating with cabinets. **Carpets and Rugs:** Carpet fibers and their characteristics. How to select the right carpet or rug. **Carports:** Ideas for making the best use of available space. **Ceilings:** Unusual ideas for decorating. Ceiling systems and how to use them. **Centers of Interest:** How to locate, use and furnish. **Closets:** How to get the most out of existing space and how to find more space. **Color:** Color facts, how to use the color wheel, types of color schemes (how to build, use, change, adapt and plan), color psychology and how it affects your everyday life. **Cooking Islands and Peninsulas:** Ideas for making the most of a large kitchen. Types and styles.

Decorating Ideas: 32 pages of bright ideas to make your home exciting and different. **Dining Areas:** How to plan, arrange and decorate. **Dishwashers:** How to select the right one for your use. **Dividers:** How to build and use as decorative devices. Bookcases and partitions. **Draperies:** How to make, step-by-step. Drapery fabrics, their characteristics and how to choose the right one for your home. **Dressing Rooms:** Ideas for lighting. **Dry Walls:** How to choose and install. Hints on foundation treatments.

Entry Halls and Entryways: How to contrive and decorate. **Exercise Rooms:** Big and small rooms. Basements and garages.

Flower Arrangements: Classic, country, contemporary, Oriental, step-by-step planning, how to dry and preserve flowers, foliage, and selecting the right tools. **Frames and Matting:** How to choose and make. **Furniture Arrangement:** How to find center of interest, define traffic lanes, arrange furniture to suit a room and your needs.

Garages: How to put space to work more effectively and how to decorate a remodeled garage.

Kitchens: Decorating, color and accessories, planning for work flow and equipment, cabinets, serving areas, window and lighting treatments, storage.

Laundry Centers: Adding them to your basement. Remodeling ideas. **Lighting:** Scale and balance, lamps, fixtures, fluorescents, mood lighting, ideas for living and dining rooms, bathrooms, bedrooms, kitchens and studies. **Living Rooms:** Decorating, arrangement, centers of interest, conversational groupings, patterns, wall and window treatments, floors and floor coverings.

Paneling: Styles, kinds, how to panel with plywood, join panels, choose and use moldings, how to panel with hardboard. **Parking and Driveways:** How to plan for greater efficiency. Tips on landscaping. **Partitions:** Decorating and space-planning with partitions. How to build them. **Party Ideas:** Ideas for special table settings, for decorating formal and informal parties, brunches and open house.

Remodeling: Ideas for all around the home, for entries and hallways, living rooms, dining areas, family rooms, bedrooms, bathrooms, kitchens and exteriors. **Resilient Flooring:** Types, where to use, how to lay a tile floor and how to lay strip floorings.

Slipcovers: How to decorate with slipcovers, choose ready-made ones, coordinate them with draperies, and make your own, step-by-step. **Storage:** Living, family and dining rooms, kitchens, bedrooms, bathrooms, miscellaneous.

Tables: Classic, country, contemporary, specialized and tables you can build. **Table Settings and Linens:** Classic, country and contemporary settings, color schemes, special occasions, how to plan for table tops, tricks with napkins, runners, place mats, special-effect linens. **Teenage rooms:** 20 pages of ideas for teens. **Television:** How to select TV coverups, and proper placement. **Terrace Tiling:** How to tile with plastic, metal or ceramic tile.

Upholstering: Types of fibers and fabrics, how to choose the right ones for your needs.

Walls and Wall Covering: Wallpaper, style and color, how to remove old wallpaper, prepare walls, hang wallpaper, select for color and special uses; fabric, cork, painted walls, how to select and install tiled walls, vinyl, carpeted, linoleum, fiberglass and brick walls. **Window Treatments:** Draperies and curtains, beads, framing, café curtains, shades and blinds, shutters and screens, problem windows, ideas for multiple, corner, strip, single, bay, radiator windows and windows of different sizes. **Woods:** How to refinish hardwood floors, remove a floor scratch, and ideas for using wood decoratively.

How To Use Your Encyclopedia

Your *Practical Encyclopedia of Good Decorating and Home Improvement* is set up for your convenience and for your immediate use.

Arranged in easy-to-follow (and easy-to-find) alphabetical order, each volume is divided into two sections. The first is referred to as the Feature section. Highlighted are major articles covering all the important facts you need to know about decorating and home improvement. And each article is fully illustrated.

The second section is called the Master/
Guide. Following immediately after the Feature section in each volume, this is a master
guide not only to your encyclopedia, but to
the whole world of decorating and home
improvement. Here you will find concise articles on influential designers and architects,
important decorating terms and styles as well
as materials used in home improvement and
decorating; also listed is every article in the
encyclopedia, along with a descriptive entry.

As a further aid to your enjoyment, in-
depth cross references are included in both
the Feature and Master/Guide sections.
These references can be found at the end of
each feature or entry.

Also, wherever possible, instructions are
provided as to where you can get a specific
Project Plan or *Home Plan* that is illustrated
in an article (see Index).

FEATURE SECTION
Here are your major home improvement and
decorating articles. Fully illustrated, they
cover practically every detail you need to
know—from step-by-step handyman instructions for such jobs as laying tile, installing
ceilings, preparing paint and painting, or upholstering to the larger home improvement
jobs, such as adding a new room or garage.

Also featured are other money-saving articles, such as those on buying and selecting
area rugs, creating the right color harmony or
a center of interest, arranging accessories for
the greatest effect, and many other action-
producing ideas you can use immediately.

Your Feature section is designed to answer
your questions and solve your decorating problems quickly. For example, let's say you have
just decorated your living room. You've chosen the right furniture, colors and so on. Still,
it lacks something that can set it apart, make
it unique and distinctive—perhaps, an accessory. What to choose? It's simple. Flip to page
46 of your Volume 1. Here, in 64 idea-packed
pages, you discover that "accessories really are
the spice of decorating."

MASTER/GUIDE
At the end of each volume, easily spotted by
the blue bar at the top of the page, is the
Master/Guide. Here are complete encyclopedia listings and identifications of decorating
and home improvement terms.

It includes pertinent information on famous
designers and architects—both historical and
contemporary—and their work as an influence
on your home. It has technical information on
such items as fabric weaves, antique porcelains, and glass. It includes historical design
terms, such as ball-and-claw foot, spoon back
chairs, plus hundreds of other entries.

Basically, your encyclopedia's aim is to
provide you with the most complete and up-
to-date information for making your home the
focal point of your life.

The Basic Guidelines You Need To Start Improving Your Home

An inviting room, a welcoming, comfortable home: these are the goals of good decorating. How to achieve them may involve a multitude of decisions on your part. But they will never become bewildering if you learn to use the basic guide lines that are set forth here.

Decorating—or redecorating—might begin from many points: a favorite color, a handsome pattern, some choice pieces of furniture you've acquired or inherited. It really doesn't matter where you start. What does matter is that you build soundly on a chosen base.

Put your personality into your home

Pleasing combinations of color, pattern and texture, with attention to scale and balance, all play a part in the creation of a beautiful room or home. Yet, they alone are not enough to produce truly memorable, completely satisfying surroundings. That other ingredient we must, for lack of a more precise term, call "personality."

Start from the personal—tastes, interests, hobbies, life patterns of you and your family. If a casual style of eating and entertaining in informal dress is what comes naturally, don't be charmed into furnishing the much-used rooms of your home with delicate fabrics, dainty patterns or fragile furniture.

If you read a great deal, collect primitive art, are an ambitious gardener, a water sports enthusiast, or gatherer of sea shells, let signs of these interests appear in the decorations of your home. Don't hide from view those things that could endow a decorating scheme with the stamp of individuality. But while the personal viewpoint is important, don't forget the professional.

The homemaker who has confidence and enjoys tracking down exactly the right furnishings may decide to do all the decorating herself. Professional decorators (commonly known as interior designers) can give expert guidance that can save time and money. They are familiar with many lines, know how to find what you want; they have learned by experience how to select the longest lasting furnishings, know where to economize and where, in the long run, it's better to pay a little more for greater satisfaction.

If you use a decorator, decide first how much you want him to do. Determine what kind of services he offers. Some offer consultation only; others will help you shop, and some will help with everything from planning to actual purchasing. You will need to itemize this information before you can arrive at any kind of budget.

Train yourself to make sound judgments on new furnishings by studying such interior designs as this one. Of each room pictured in this encyclopedia that has appeal for you, ask yourself what elements account for the total effect. What parts were played by color, pattern, style, and texture.

Here, the distinctive architectural design of the room was a primary factor influencing the selection of furnishings. To emphasize the appeal of a spacious room and the charm of a high, beamed ceiling, off-white was used for all background areas: floors, walls, and window treatment.

But to inject life into the scheme, generous accents of rich red and gold were introduced. For the something dark needed to contrast with large areas of light, neutral color, the dark stained beams, slate hearth, coffee table, and the lamp base on the red lacquer table were imaginatively introduced.

Whether you decide to be your own interior decorator or to engage the help of a professional, it still behooves you to increase your understanding of basic principles of design. By improving your knowledge of how color, scale, pattern and texture operate, you will be far better able to choose between the variety of possible choices of furnishings.

It is the main purpose of this volume and those to follow to help you grow in your ability to make wise decorating decisions. And quite as important, to help you discover the many ways in which your individuality and your family's can be projected upon the furnishings and decorations of your home. To do this effectively is, in fact, the secret behind all really great decorating.

How to understand your needs

There is a saying that "nothing important ever 'just happens.' Somebody makes it happen." In decorating and home improvement this is true. And that somebody will be you if you begin all major and minor decorating projects by analyzing the needs of your family. Regardless of the size of the task—one room or seven rooms—you still need to think through the requirements of each person in the home.

If the whole family's involved, ask each member old enough to participate actively to list the added facilities, conveniences, attractiveness he or she wants as a result of the changes contemplated.

Does the man of the family need a desk in a quiet corner where he can work undisturbed? Does he have a hobby that requires work and storage space? Is one child a serious musician, another younger and often noisy, a host to groups of small friends? Should plans include the provision of soundproof areas or separate quarters? Do you dream of a kitchen office for planning menus, storing cookbooks, payment of monthly bills?

All these and many more needs—as they're pertinent to your family—should be set down on paper, kept in mind as your plans for a decorating project proceed.

How to decide on style and color

Once you've established your family's needs, decide on the style of furnishings that will best suit your present way of living. In a small home that includes young children, casual furnishings are probably the soundest choice. If there's room for both living room largely reserved to adult use and family room that teen-agers might use for their kind of entertaining, you may want to decorate the living room in a formal style not chosen primarily for durability.

Color, too, is somewhat dependent upon the kind of use the room or rooms are to receive, and the color schemes of adjacent rooms. They, too, should be taken into consideration. Perhaps you'll decide to have one basic scheme throughout. If not, you will still want harmony from room to room wherever one is visible from another.

If your decorating concern at the moment is primarily with the bedrooms, take into consideration the color preferences of your family. If these preferences are impractical as basic colors, discover ways to work them into your scheme as accents. For further help on color and style, see the following pages.

Sharply contrasting textural qualities are a dominant theme in ▶ the decoration of this family room with raised dining platform at one end. Smooth textures predominate in wood-paneled walls, copper fireplace hood, leather-like upholstery fabric; and their appeal is heightened by juxtaposition with roughness of fireplace brick and soft nap of red carpeting.

Color plays a less important role than texture, but cheerful accents of red and gold floor coverings, red and deep green upholstery on chairs, red accents in wall decorations and in the inviting bowl of apples add to the total appeal, as do the green plants on the table in the foreground and the larger Norfolk Island Pine given floor placement.

A window treatment that uses interior shutters of wood and dispenses with draperies is appropriate to total style and in keeping with the simplicity established by architectural lines.

Color

Color in its thousands of mutations is the keystone of home furnishings, binding together all the elements of decorating. Color can bring about a metamorphosis in a room, giving it warmth, vitality, and beauty.

But how to choose from the multitude of colors? How to use them creatively? The language of color is not difficult to learn. Terminology is often used loosely. So it's a good idea to start out with accurate definitions.

How to use the color wheel
The color wheel is actually nature's rainbow bent to make a circle.

A color wheel is a helpful guide in selecting a color scheme. It enables you to see at a glance the colors, their families, and their complements or opposites. By studying the wheel, you can visualize how each color will look with another, and which colors can be mixed to produce new ones.

Black, white, and gray also affect color. White intensifies, while black absorbs, the color of objects seen against it. Black also has the ability to unify colors, and to effect harmony in schemes that combine many bright hues. Gray works much like a shadow on outdoor color—it tends to subdue colors adjacent to it.

When light is passed through a prism, the white rays of sunlight separate into distinct hues, as in the rainbow. Almost everything around us has the capacity to absorb one or more of these beams. Rays that are not absorbed are reflected to the eye and make up the color we see. Grass on a hillside, for instance, absorbs red rays and reflects the blue and yellow, making it appear green.

There are a number of systems for classifying colors, but the one most commonly used is the color wheel based on three: red, yellow, and blue. Any other color is made by mixing these hues.

There are also three created by mixing equal parts of one primary color with another: red and yellow make orange; red plus blue is violet; and blue plus yellow makes green.

By mixing each color of the large flower petals, opposite, with its neighbor, you get: yellow-orange, red-orange, red-violet, blue-violet, blue-green, and yellow-green. This mixing can go on indefinitely.

Color terms you should understand
To speak with authority, you need to know a few terms that will help you describe the exact color you want to use.

Hue refers to a particular name of a color, such as red or orange. Value has to do with a color's lightness or darkness. Colors that are nearer white in value are called tints and colors that are closer to black in color are called shades.

Monochromatic schemes—those that use only one color, its ▶ own values and intensities—are usually appealing and harmonious. Here, a monochromatic scheme in green, with accents of black and white, calls on pattern and texture to keep it lively.

Nature's changing palette offers us rich examples for the monochromatic schemes, since nothing in nature is all of a color. Look closely at a grassy bank and you will see not one hue but countless gradations of the color green. For information on "complementary" schemes, see next page.

Color has another dimension called intensity or tone. This refers to brightness or dullness. A peacock's tail and a garden pea are both green, yet the two tones are very different. The peacock feathers are in clear, intense colors, whereas the pea is a dull, grayish-green.

How to achieve pleasing color schemes

Combining two or more hues in harmonious relationship results in a pleasing color scheme. Once you know the principles, assembling colors will prove both challenging and pleasurable. Monochromatic schemes use only one color, but utilize a range of values and intensities. In a monochromatic room scheme the base color and one or two variations of it, plus some neutralizing black and white, make a livable, easy-to-take setting. This kind of color scheme is restful, and makes a good background for accessories.

A high-back settee of wood stained dark green replaces two more conventional chairs in this eating area. Area rug of cardinal red, checked red-green fabric on dining chairs, accent pillows carry out a pleasingly executed complementary scheme. Colors used here coordinate with hues of an adjoining kitchen.

A related scheme combines hues that are side by side on the color wheel—ones that have a common color denominator, as yellow-green, yellow, and yellow-orange. These related schemes, too, are generally restful and refreshing. They gain interest by variation in value and intensity.

A complementary scheme uses opposites on the color wheel, such as blue and orange. Contrasting colors are lively and vibrant, but it's best to let one color dominate. A vivid color and its complement can be quieted, if you prefer, by graying them, or reducing their values.

This brings us to another dimension of color. Split the color wheel vertically and you'll see that all hues fall into one of two groups—warm and cool colors. The warm, sun colors reflect all the energy of sun and earth, and add a feeling of conviviality to any room. The tangy reds, yellows, and oranges are ideal for rooms with exposures on the north or east.

The cool side of the wheel is made up of evening hues of blue, green, and violet. These jewel-like colors are basically restful and soothing. They are good choices for rooms with a southern or western exposure that get a lot of sun.

Use both warm and cool tones in your planning. Temper either group with liberal amounts of neutrals, and with accents from the other side of the palette.

How light affects color

Color becomes capricious under changing light conditions. As light falls on a colored surface, it affects its appearance in several ways.

Walls of rough-sawn cedar stained dark green and quarry tile ▶ flooring of red-orange hue are paired in a kitchen of rustic styling. Chair seat pads repeat the warm tones of flooring. Again, as in the dining area pictured across the page, complementary colors are coordinated with those adjacent areas.

When you plan a decorating scheme, you'll need to consider the amount, intensity, and direction of natural light in a room. Note the size, number, and direction of the windows. Exposures on the north and east get cool light, while those on the south and west get direct sunlight for more hours of the day. These factors should influence your selection.

Optical illusion causes some strange color effects that can often be used to advantage. For instance, any color appears much brighter when used in a large area, so in choosing a wall color select a slightly less intense tone than you actually want; it will look brighter on the wall.

Yellow, orange, and red posies underfoot, on a ground of neutral off-white, are keyed to the warm yellow of dining room draperies and to the red in the stripes of the chair-seat upholstery. The color value of the rug is played to the full.

How to assemble your color scheme

To be successful, a color scheme must be a source of pleasure for you and your family and at the same time be suited to the room and its uses. Consider the physical aspects of the room—its function, size, exposure, and lighting—in your plans.

Now turn back to the color wheel and choose one color as a starting point. Decide which type of scheme will best suit your needs, and select several companion colors for the major hue. In your early efforts at building a scheme, it's a good idea to limit yourself to three or four colors. It takes a practiced hand to bring off a multihued scheme successfully.

Since the walls constitute the largest area of color in a room, choose this color first. Quiet colors for large areas live best, and are not so quickly tiring as bolder hues. You can often use a grayed tone of your favorite color for walls, and perhaps for the floor covering, too.

The second color, or colors, can be a bit brighter. Large upholstered pieces, and often the draperies, fall into this category. The sharp colors that accent the others normally make up a small percentage of the total color in the room. Reserve them for pillows, lamps, pictures, and other decorative accessories.

The sloping ceilings of an A-frame structure can be a claustrophobic, head-bumping buisance or, if handled properly, they can be the room's biggest asset, as witnessed by the attic-study retreat at the left.

The successful color scheme is the most important ingredient of this room at the top. At first glance, this room may appear to be all one color—brown—and one might be baffled as to what color or colors should be used. A working knowledge of the basic color wheel easily provides the answer.

The room at the left was decorated using a complementary color scheme. Complementary colors are those colors directly opposite each other on the color wheel—red-green, blue-orange, and yellow-violet. Here, the designer balanced the rich red and orange tones of the wood with the cool evening hues of blue and green. In a variety of intensity and value, a small amount of these cool colors was able to quiet the vast expanse of warm wood tones, and because cool colors create distance, visually heighten the ceiling.

Scale

The furnishings of this charming corner of a room have been selected with exactly the opposite set of goals in mind from those that guided the choice of the generously proportioned pieces in the inviting room pictured across the page.

Here we have a fairly small space that we do not wish to look cramped. Notice that the pattern of the wall covering is delicate in size, neat and—in part—geometrical. Imagine, if you will, what would have been the result had a large, splashy flowered pattern been placed there in its stead. The wallcovering and the furniture have been chosen for their delicate appearance.

Both desk and chair seem smaller than they really are because they have slim legs, do not present a solid visual block that reaches clear to the floor—as do the sofa and chair in the room opposite. They are not really exceptionally small pieces, but they appear to be smaller and lighter than they are because of their lines and their "up-off-the-floor" looks.

Finally, the same "see through" quality makes the table lamp look smaller than it is.

Like the water that's never missed till a well runs dry, scale is seldom noticed if it is competently handled in room furnishings.

Scale, in essence, has to do with the size of things in relation to the size of their surroundings. Most people are aware of its importance in clothes selection—even though they may not know that they're observing the laws of "scale." But we may be a little less knowledgeable when it comes to selecting home furnishings whose size relates well to the size of their planned placement.

Scale is basic to good decorating

Scale refers both to the total form and mass of the object, and its relationship to the size of the room. Scale is also the relationship of each piece as compared to the size of other furniture in the same room.

If you're of the newlywed set living in a tiny apartment, stop considering (for the moment) the purchase of an enormous overstuffed sofa. Instead, look for a piece with slim lines or, maybe, settle for a love seat that can move to the master bedroom when you buy a house.

But if your home—or some of its rooms—are of heroic proportions, think several times before purchasing dainty little gilt chairs (unless, of course, these can be placed in a room that suits their scale).

In this large, handsome room, furnishings "on the grand ▶ scale" are not only appropriate; they are necessary. Notice how well the very large hanging light fixture suits the space assigned it. In a tiny room, its effect would be ludicrous. But here it performs its good lighting function perfectly.

The table lamp, too, is big—in "scale" with the big room it helps to light and decorate. A large sofa and generously proportioned lounge chair are equally well chosen for appropriate positions in a comfortably spacious room.

In addition to actual size, there is a visual factor to be recognized when you consider the matter of choosing furnishings that will be in scale with surroundings. It is a fact that a solid piece, such as the overstuffed sofa, appears to be larger than a sofa of the same length and width but of a different and less solid style—one set up on slim legs, and not upholstered but fitted with tailored, slim appearing cushions for back and seat. The color, too, is important. Dark hues bulk larger visually than pale ones.

Style

Freedom of choice in furnishings today is unparalleled. Many designs are indebted to the past; others are as new as tomorrow.

Nine major style influences on furniture

To help eliminate some of the confusion about style names and antecedents, here's a look at the nine major influences that are most significant contributors to the design of today's furniture. They are: French, English, Italian, Oriental, Spanish, American Traditional, German, Scandinavian, and American Modern.

Across the page you see a room furnished largely in styles first popular in past centuries. On pages immediately following you will see rooms that are furnished in blends of several styles in a manner known as "eclectic."

Later on in this volume—and in subsequent volumes of this encyclopedia—you will find entries dealing separately with most of the periods and specific furniture styles we mention here only in passing. As you study this and following volumes, notice styles of furniture, blends that appeal.

Furniture styling tends to follow social history. In past centuries, furniture was made by cabinetmakers serving royal courts or by country craftsmen who translated the elegant court styles into crude but pleasant provincial adaptations.

Traditional styles often took their names from reigning monarchs or monarchies: Louis XV, Queen Anne, Jacobean. Or they borrowed their names from styles of government—Directoire, Regency. Country styles are usually named for their place of origin: Italian or French Provincial, English Country, or Early American.

Few can afford the truly authentic antiques, but all can have the handsome reproductions and adaptations of earlier designs that are available in today's furniture.

Most American contemporary designs, such as those that furnish the room below, seek to be functional, avoid adornment, hope to achieve beauty through the lines of the piece itself rather than through its decorations. They often use laminated plastic tops as further evidence of concern for the functional.

Furnishings of this inviting dining room are hearty English ▶ Country—a Welsh cupboard loaded with plates, pewter, brass; a tavern table; and high-back Windsor chairs. Decorating is strong and forceful to add punch to the scheme; witness the wide expanse of powerful pattern in the curvy, stencil-like wallpaper. Still in the mood of the furnishings, but with a nod to today's desire for low-care floors, is the resilient vinyl that looks like polished wood planks and red bricks.

How to use the eclectic style

Near the turn of the century, Marconi was successful in establishing wireless contact across the English Channel—a distance of only 32 miles. Today, we can communicate with astronauts in space. In the years that have passed since that first trans-channel signal, there have been revolutionary advances in architecture and interior design. The style pendulum has swung from Victorian over-decoration, through the early days of functional "modern," to a nostalgic return of the softened line and subdued ornamentation.

Furnishings in an eclectic style are drawn from many sources. Ideally, only the best and truest are taken from each source and combined into a satisfying whole. As American families are more traveled, more knowledgeable, and more sophisticated in a style sense than in the past, eclecticism is a natural outgrowth. The days of buying an all-of-a-kind "suite" of furniture are past; this is an era of mixing styles, periods, materials.

Our present eclecticism does not, however, reflect an interest in mere acquisition of oddments and fragments of styles. There is a genuine desire, particularly among the young, to acquire furniture and accessories to express their individuality.

In buying furniture, today's younger homemakers want more than a style label; they want an understanding of antecedents.

It follows that while there is freedom to choose the best, there is also inherent danger in eclecticism. It must be carefully controlled to be successful, or it will result in a confusion of miscellany. Control can be accomplished by the wise use of color, arrangement, and background. Singly and together, these decorating elements can unify seemingly unrelated furnishings in a harmonious whole. A play of rich color against neutralizing white can be the catalyst, as in the interesting room pictured opposite.

There is a time-honored affinity between basically English styles and Oriental motifs and designs. The English were, after all, responsible for adapting for European use much that was good in Chinese art—especially as it concerned home furnishings. Chippendale is the name we remember for the borrowings from Oriental designs. The eclecticism of the room below reflects this.

The sophisticated combination of primitive with cultured ▶ designs is a good example of the eclecticism that appeals to so many of today's homemakers. They have traveled to many lands, seen and appreciated a wide variety of art styles, enjoy decorating their homes with pieces that are both a pleasant reminder of their travels, and an artistic addition to the decorative or functional furnishings of their homes.

Neutral background, clever grouping make this collection of decorative pieces artistically satisfying. Contrast of sleek sofas and crudely fashioned coffee table is appealing.

There are many patterns in the room shown below. The woodwork forms a pattern. The floors, curtains, rug, and the arrangement of the furniture—all are a part of the pattern scheme.

The wallpaper chosen for this room looks right. Let's examine why. In the first place, it is in scale with the rest of the furnishings in the room. The pattern is not too large, neither is it too small. It unifies and provides background.

The design elements in the wallpaper do not appear spotty. They form a rhythmic repetition of color-blocks and are closely woven together. The contrast between the colors used in the paper is not too pronounced. The two most prominent colors in the wallpaper are subdued and subtle. They look well together, and they pick up the color of the woodwork in the hallway and ceiling beams. Notice that the series of different squares in the wallpaper complements the block design of the flooring. This creates a feeling of harmony. And this harmony is restated by the lines of the wood paneling and of the wood beams. The curtains at the window in the hallway are made from a fabric that matches the wallpaper. Although a plain fabric that blended with the color of the wallpaper would also be suitable, the use of matching fabric gives a more unified effect.

There are no pictures on the walls. But although it is difficult to hang pictures against a patterned wallpaper, it is possible to use other accessories. Here a clock has been mounted on the wall of the stairway, and two ornaments hang on the living-room wall.

Pattern and texture

The total design of a room is composed of an interplay of color, pattern, texture, and shape. All these elements together create a kind of rhythm born of repetition. In music, the pleasantest rhythms have much repetition. And each piece of music is dependent on all its parts being balanced—if the total effect required is melodious. The rhythm of a room is developed in much the same way. Pattern creates interest or counterpoint. A room without pattern is apt to be monotonous. And yet, with too much pattern, a room can look restless.

There are many rules about how much pattern should be used in a room. Some say one-third of a room should have pattern; others say one-fourth; still others claim the classic Greek proportion is the right one—two parts emphasis to three parts rest. They are all right—on occasion. Use with discretion.

Pattern is like spice in cooking. Use it with the same sort of care and discretion. Get acquainted with its basic requirements. Learn to recognize repetition of shape and line. Discover how to use subtle variations of pattern effectively. Search for ways to use variation as accent.

Find out how to select a wallpaper that stays in the background when that's what you need; how to choose a paper that suits the size of your room and its furnishings; how to pick one that is intended to introduce an accent of bold designs or bright color when that's what you need.

Recognize how to pick out patterns for furniture that are appropriate to its design. Learn how to choose florals that have at least two things in common with the rest of your room—color and size. Get to know how pattern provides diversity and builds interest.

Bold zebra-striped upholstery fabric generates the excitement in this striking setting. The color scheme here is composed of almost equal amounts of black, white, and red. Something was needed to provide a daring splash in the room. The swirling stripes are appropriate. They repeat the lines in the wicker furniture. They seem to move in the same way, and are unified through their color with the rest of the room.

The upholstery fabric also illustrates an important design concept called transition. The lines formed by the black decorative strips on the wall, the lamps, and the fireplace are mainly vertical. The frame of the furniture, glass table, and the polka dots in the red rug suggest roundness. An equal amount of straight and round lines might seem unpleasant except for the transitional curving lines of the upholstery and vases. They provide another kind of line that unites shapes.

The movement of these curving lines is pleasant to the eye. Such lines are often found in patterns to bring together the various parts of a design. This technique has been applied to the decorating of this room scheme.

Thought was also given to the interplay of texture in the treatment of this room. Texture, like pattern, helps make a room more interesting. There are basically three kinds of texture—coarse, fine, and medium. Within reason, combinations of textures can be used. Coarse- and fine-textured materials do not look right together. The difference between them is too great. Medium textures can be used with either coarse or fine ones. The use of texture is also governed by the scale of the other furnishings. In this room, the shaggy cotton terry fabric on the upholstered furniture provides contrast with the many smooth and shiny surfaces.

Room arrangement

Every family has unique needs and desires for its home, and the way to secure a home to satisfy those needs and desires is through planning. No plan will suit everyone. The process of planning, however, is much the same, whatever your goals. You must make a series of decisions that will produce a home incorporating your requirements, reflecting your tastes.

The object of planning is to get the most convenience, comfort, and beauty with the least cost. The first step is to sit down with your family and decide on basic needs and feasible budget. Include the children in planning sessions that concern them. They pop up with unexpectedly workable suggestions.

Then, when you have determined your main objectives, begin looking for ideas that can help you obtain your goals. Look up references in these volumes that apply to the job you want done. For example, when you start a kitchen remodeling project, look up *Additions* and *Remodeling*. Then check under *Kitchens, Cabinets, Cooking Islands, Breakfast Rooms, Buffets, Lighting, Refrigerators, Ranges,* and *Storage*. The secret of good planning is research, so use your encyclopedia as a library.

Examine blueprints or make scale drawings to be sure plans are right for you. Sketch in your furniture to determine what new pieces you need and what to leave out. And experiment. Your first attempt at room arrangement will probably not turn up the best design. Only with practice do you become perfect.

The house plan shown on these pages illustrates the benefits of making complete drawings. In the bedroom area on the upper level, beds, dressers, chairs, and tables have been drawn to scale and set in place. The circles on the tables and dressers represent lamps. You can see, for example, that there is enough room for a lamp in the middle bedroom between the bed and the closet on the one side, and between the bed and dressers on the other. You also find that the desk section of the furniture built under the window must be on the right side.

Measure those pieces of furniture you have and see how they will fit in the new room. Incorporate in your plans the lighting each room requires. Study storage areas to determine what should be placed in each; which is best for linens, which for out-of-season clothing, etc.

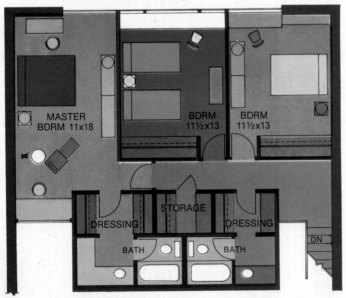

UPPER LEVEL

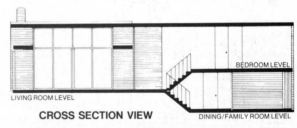

CROSS SECTION VIEW

LIVING ROOM LEVEL
BEDROOM LEVEL
DINING/FAMILY ROOM LEVEL

This cross-sectional view shows different levels of this particular house plan. A view such as this helps you to visualize the relationships between the levels. It might also suggest some problems that would not be so apparent in another view. For example, in this plan the bedrooms are directly above the dining and family rooms. You may have television viewers or piano-playing members of your family downstairs while young children are sleeping upstairs. A plan will suggest changing this arrangement. Also, a few dollars spent here to insure good soundproofing may solve your problem and prove a wise investment.

Use elevations that show the outside of your house or addition to help plan what landscaping you need.

On your plans, also include the dimensions of the windows. These measurements will help you create accurately the window treatments you want for each room.

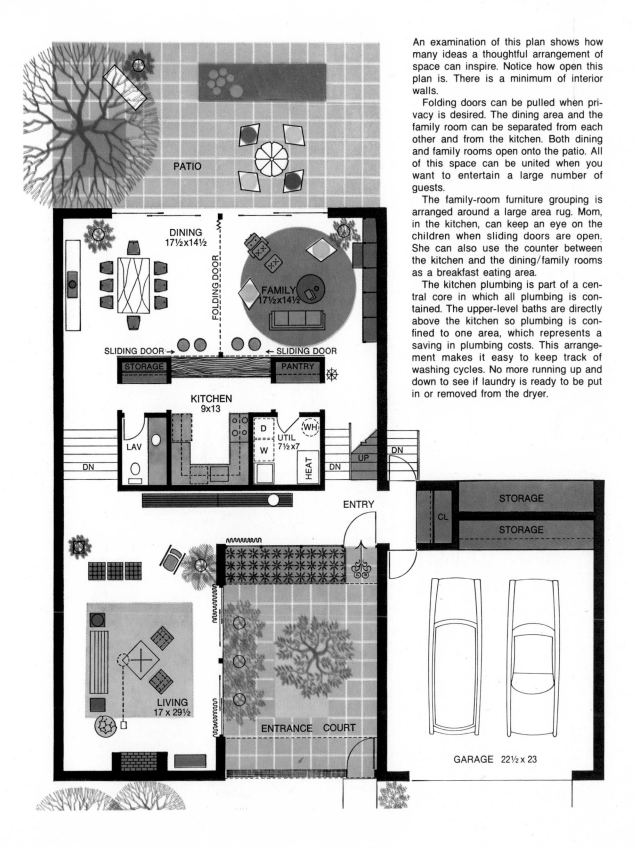

PATIO

DINING
17½x14½

FOLDING DOOR

FAMILY
17½x14½

SLIDING DOOR →   ← SLIDING DOOR

STORAGE   PANTRY

KITCHEN
9x13

LAV

D   WH
UTIL
7½x7
W   HEAT

DN

DN   UP   DN

ENTRY

CL

STORAGE

STORAGE

LIVING
17 x 29½

ENTRANCE   COURT

GARAGE   22½ x 23

An examination of this plan shows how many ideas a thoughtful arrangement of space can inspire. Notice how open this plan is. There is a minimum of interior walls.

Folding doors can be pulled when privacy is desired. The dining area and the family room can be separated from each other and from the kitchen. Both dining and family rooms open onto the patio. All of this space can be united when you want to entertain a large number of guests.

The family-room furniture grouping is arranged around a large area rug. Mom, in the kitchen, can keep an eye on the children when sliding doors are open. She can also use the counter between the kitchen and the dining/family rooms as a breakfast eating area.

The kitchen plumbing is part of a central core in which all plumbing is contained. The upper-level baths are directly above the kitchen so plumbing is confined to one area, which represents a saving in plumbing costs. This arrangement makes it easy to keep track of washing cycles. No more running up and down to see if laundry is ready to be put in or removed from the dryer.

Floors

For the major rooms of any home, it's a safe bet you'll spend more on the floors and floor coverings than you will on any other one item of furnishing. But that initially expensive floor covering, if wisely chosen, will also outlast almost all other furnishings, require only cleaning to keep it fresh and new looking for years.

Today's floor coverings come in such variety that it beggars description to tell of them all. Here is a summary of the major types. Later, under suitable entries, you'll read more details about all major varieties, see many examples of effective ways to use them.

The big "split" is between hard and soft surface floorings. Traditionally, hard surface flooring (tile or sheet form) has been put in kitchens, bathrooms, family or recreation rooms, and occasionally in entries. Carpets and rugs have been thought of, until recently, as appropriate for living and dining rooms, bedrooms, stairs, and halls.

But today there is an array of specialized carpets that go into kitchens and bathrooms, that behave beautifully because of a waterproof barrier between synthetic fiber top and a bottom layer of rubber, foam, or other spongy material. The nap feels good underfoot and serves as a welcome absorber of sound.

Resilient flooring, of which this is a handsome example, comes in two basic forms. You may buy tiles, which are cemented in place to serve as a permanent floor. Or, you can choose sheet materials, which are usually cemented permanently. Occasionally the sheet materials adapt for use as rugs, and these are loose-laid, often in apartments and in rented homes, to be moved later.

Tiles lend themselves to do-it-yourself installation. Self-adhesive varieties are especially easy to use. One company has simplified the task so that, although you still have to prepare the subfloor for the adhesive, you no longer have to apply adhesive to the entire floor—only to perimeters and seams of tile.

Sheet vinyl, a favorite for kitchens and family rooms, has the virtue of no seams—no places for dirt to catch and collect. There are marvelous colors and patterns available. Many are cushioned to add extra resilience. Some types must be installed by experts; others may be scissor-cut to fit and laid in place.

Good decorating often starts with floor covering, and when it ▶ is lively pumpkin-colored wall-to-wall carpeting, it might well inspire the choice of remaining room furnishings in a bedroom-study such as this. Draperies and bedspread are color keyed to carpeting.

Unless you intend your floor to be a focal part of decorating, you'll choose from solid colors or subdued patterns. Bold patterns in floor covering restrict you pretty much to solids everywhere else if you're to avoid a disturbingly busy look.

Carpeting and rugs come in many colors, textures, sizes, and qualities. Your budget will partly determine your choice, but it's poor economy to buy floor covering that wears out rapidly, cleans poorly, flattens down to show traffic patterns.

Walls

There's no larger area of color in any room than its four walls and ceiling. This mass of color sets the stage for furnishings if used cleverly.

With today's innovations in materials and designs, walls become more than an expanse of space on which to display an accessory or two. As part of the room's background, they should complement its furnishings—but they can do more.

Walls can be the dominating feature of room decor. They can draw attention away from awkward architectural features (if you learn the basics of camouflage), visually change the size and shape of a room, and provide the focal point for furniture arrangement.

They can be plain, wallpapered, covered with fabric, tile, leather, or treated as part of the room's architecture with brick, stone or

The wall, when it is treated as part of the room's architecture, as is this one of brick, with the mortar purposely left somewhat rough, becomes a dominant feature in decorating. Here, since the color of the brick acts as a neutral background, a mass of color must be employed elsewhere in the room's furnishings. Bright blue in upholstery fabric, rug, and painting was a good choice. Style of furnishings is also vital, since exposed brick rules out dainty-looking pieces. Soft texture of upholstery is all the more attractive in contrast with roughness of brick wall.

wood. They can also serve to store many objects in attractive fashion, combining function and decoration effectively.

Special treatments in wall coverings as borders, dadoes, contrasting trims, murals, and *trompe l'oeil* designs can enlarge and enhance both walls and furnishings. These special effects will be treated at length in later sections of this and following volumes of this encyclopedia. Look at wall treatments in pictures throughout for new ideas you can use in decorating.

In planning wall coverings, decide first on your goal. Is the room small or large? What will be its use? Are there flaws to hide? Many solutions are available. Small rooms look bigger if woodwork matches walls; cut-up areas look less so when colors and patterns are carried from one room to the next. Murals can push walls out visually.

Dark hues reduce the size of very large areas; light ones seem to expand dimensions of tiny ones. Big patterns shrink apparent space; small ones make it seem larger.

Walls can do much more than stand there and be decorative, if you use them properly. They are functional, too, especially when treated as this one is, with its bright red color showing through open areas; shelves, doors, and drawers are painted a soft yellow to match the floor for a two-color room scheme.

Count the things this wall does: it houses a television set, stores books, provides a desk with pigeonhole compartments above writing surface, displays a variety of art objects (including a large painting) and also accommodates a variety of possessions not on view, behind its flush-construction doors.

Windows

Our ancestors once regarded windows as a means of letting light and air into their dwellings. If the view was good, so much the better; but beauty came far after use in their thinking.

Today, with artificial light, and furnaces and air conditioners to give us whatever temperature we choose, the windows of our homes have become more important for their decorative potential than at any time in history.

In older homes with architectural lines similar to those of the room pictured opposite, we may find that the best way to capitalize upon windows is to dress them in styles and fabrics that make them a focal point of our total decorating scheme, an opportunity to use color and pattern with a fairly lavish hand.

Modern architecture frequently uses windows to expand apparent living space, and to serve as a picture on a giant scale. The room below is in this group. The type of window you have affects its treatment. Here are common types:

Double hung: moveable upper, lower sashes.
Casement: double- or single-sash windows that swing in or out to open or close.
Bay and bow: three or more windows or one large window that forms recess in a wall.
Jalousie: window of horizontal glass strips that adjust to various angles when open.
Clerestory: small windows near the ceiling that usually follow the roof line.

Draperies in this room, although they are attractive because of their gracefully generous folds when closed, their contrast of light against dark floor, ceiling, and woodwork when open, are important for their function: to control light. When sunlight is unpleasantly brilliant, they stop glare. When night makes privacy desirable they shut out unwanted observers.

Fabrics from which draperies such as these may be made include the natural fibers—cotton, silk, and wool—as well as the many synthetics that fall into seven categories: acetate, acrylic, modacrylic, glass fiber, nylon, polyester, and rayon.

The problem which faced the designer in this master bedroom was how to bring the two side-by-side windows into the room's spacious decor.

He could have used a single ceiling-high drapery which would have masked the windows, created height, and effectively made the windows part of a new wall. Or he could have hung window-top curtains.

Instead, the designer chose to decorate the windows with ceiling-high draperies separated by colorfully patterned pull-down shades. The feeling of spaciousness is there, but so too is an individual treatment for each window. Now, instead of unbalancing the room, the windows help round out the color scheme and become an integral part of the decor.

Top. Put your walls to work. Make them do something besides just hold the ceiling in place. Wall coverings quickly and easily give any room in the house an unmistakable personality and mood. Here, a flower-patterned, vinyl wall covering transforms an ordinary bathroom into an enviable bouquet. It is pretty and practical as well, because vinyl is washable and durable enough to withstand daily wear and tear.

Bottom. With a little imagination, walls can do much more than act as a background for the room's furnishings. A wall can be the dominating point of a room, a camouflage for architectural mistakes, or the focal point for furniture arrangement. This Scotch plaid fabric may have been used as a wall covering for any number of reasons. Perhaps the wall was badly cracked or the room's focal point needed emphasis.

Fabrics and
wall coverings

The pendulum swings again. Throughout history, walls have always been either lavishly ornate or austerely stark.

The Stone Age man invented wall coverings when he painted figures on his cave. Around 5000 B.C., Egyptian pharaohs decorated their walls with huge mosaics of ceramic tile. In China, wallpaper entered the scene about 200 B.C. During all this time wall coverings had only an aesthetic purpose. Castle living changed this. Royalty of the Middle Ages found castles damp and drafty, and began using fabric wall coverings for insulation as well as ornamentation.

With the colonization of America, homes reflected a more simple way of living. Solid whitewashed walls took over. As affluency flourished, so did decoration, and heavily patterned wallpaper became stylish. Its popularity remained until almost twenty years ago, when wallpaper was discarded for gallons of pastel paint. Recently wall coverings again have become in vogue. Now the list includes leather, aluminum foil, and plastic.

Top Left. The plastics explosion in the home furnishings world has produced a never-before freedom for both professional and do-it-yourself home decorators. Only in the past two or three years have designers' imaginations been challenged by such beautiful and versatile material as this spun-bond olefin wall covering. It is as supple as paper, yet washable and non-tearable.

Top Right. One of the real beauties of these engineered plastics is that they can be made into whatever the designer has in mind. Today we recognize plastic for its own value and no longer demand that it be a cheap imitation of an already existent material. Nearly flashing with innovation, this eye-popping geometric wall covering of fabric-backed vinyl can carry its weight in any competition.

Middle Left. No one today considers plastic a low-cost substitute. Instead, plastic is being used for its own characteristics. Because it is easy to handle, easy to apply, and easy to maintain, plastic makes a perfect material for wall coverings. A stylized poppy design in a paper-backed vinyl wall covering permits easy living in a fun-filled style perfect for today's mood.

Middle Right. Today's plastic wall coverings can be a whole new way of life. An almost endless variety of patterns, colors, and textures makes it possible to change a room's personality as often as the seasons. Applied with adhesive, many may be stripped off and reused at a later date or in another room. In addition to being mobile, this striped pattern is also flameproof.

Lower Left. A combination of the finest styles, colors, patterns, textures, and material characteristics makes plastic wall coverings perfect for today's way of life. Ideal for the "do-your-own-thing" decorating buff is this paper-backed vinyl wall covering. A direct contrast of shiny white on glossy black patent vinyl creates a new fashion look in home furnishings, the "wet" look. No matter what look you like, consider the plastics.

Lower Right. Wall coverings are the easiest way to give immediate expression to your personality in a room. Say it muted and meek, bright and bold, or anywhere in between. The choice is yours when you select any of the many styles of vinyl. This blend of Verel and rayon is expressive, but it also has the unstated qualities of being flame-retardant and sun-resistant.

Lighting

Every well-planned room has three major types of lighting: background (often called general or fill-in light), local, and accent light. Used together, the three give balanced illumination that is restful to the eye, flattering to furnishings.

Background lighting bathes the walls in soft, general illumination, ideal for relaxing or watching television. Reading, sewing, card playing and hobby activities demand good local as well as background illumination. This can be supplied by a table lamp, floor lamp, or suspended wall or ceiling fixture placed closed to the user. These must be designed to cast their light on the work surface, not in the eyes.

Before you choose your fixtures for artificial lighting, first assess the natural light. Take advantage of it to emphasize the beauty of your home; then supplement it with artificial light as needed.

Lamps attached to the end walls of built-in bookcases serve a double function of providing good reading light for persons seated on the sofa below, and of focusing attention—with light—on the large painting that acts as a major decorative feature, prominently placed just over the sofa. Height of the lamp placement guarantees no glare for readers.

Two sources of light here supplement each other attractively: overhead fixture above dining table is both decorative and functional in illuminating the table surface; the concealed lighting, which has been installed at the top of cupboards running along one wall, supplies general light and highlights art objects displayed there. When installing general lighting of this kind, it is worth the investment to have it on a rheostat which permits increasing and diminishing intensity.

In a modern home, clerestory windows at ceiling level permit ▶ good natural lighting, even when draperies must be pulled over the major portion of the window wall. Recessed lighting set into the ledge that overhangs the bookcase wall supplies excellent general illumination for the room at large.

Table, floor, and wall lamps, such as the one you see in the left foreground, supply light for a specific location—nearest chair, here—as well as increasing the overall light level.

How To Select And Use The Proper Abrasive For Each Home Improvement

An abrasive is a substance that is used to grind, wear down, scour, smooth, clean, or polish by passing over an object. There are mineral and manufactured abrasives.

The most common are backed onto paper as is sandpaper or, with the artificially manufactured glass, glass paper. Others are bonded with cement, as in a grinding wheel, or used in block form, as a pumice stone, or crushed steel for stone cutting.

Abrasives may be used to polish, or to grind metal, stone, wood, and leather, or for cutting, drilling or boring materials.

Nowadays, not only does the handyman use an abrasive, the housewife does, too. Manufactured abrasives appear in the kitchen as powders or cleansers. Steel wool is an abrasive and so, too, are the wide variety of powdered cleansers. They contain a crushed rock or shell, which is mixed with detergent. Thus they abrade and cleanse at the same time.

It is an abrasive that is used to give a manufactured object its high polish.

The color of coated abrasives helps differentiate them. From the left in this picture are: red crocus cloth for use on metals: dark gray silicon carbide for soft metals and glass; reddish garnet for sanding wood; black emery for polishing soft metals; brownish aluminum oxide for woods, metals, and sharpening tools; and yellowish-white flint for sanding paint and gummy woods.

Standard backings for abrasives include both paper and cloth types. Classification of paper backs are: "A," which is light in weight, and "C" and "D," which are heavy enough for hand or machine sanding. Cloth-backed abrasives have different alphabetical classification guides. "J" is lighter and more flexible than "X," which is used for shaping. Grit sizes are shown on the back of the sheet.

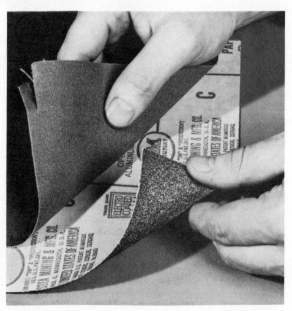

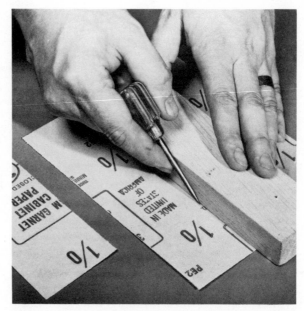

The coating applied to the paper or cloth backing may be either an open or closed one. The normal coating is close-packed, hence "closed." It contains more abrasive particles per square inch and cuts faster. The open coating shows a slight separation between grains. It cuts more slowly but doesn't clog as quickly. Emery, flint, and garnet are natural abrasives. Aluminum oxide and silicon carbide are artificial.

Cutting sandpaper with kitchen shears tends to bring on family tension. The right way to cut sandpaper to size is with a straightedge and a scratch or brad awl. Place the paper face down and score the paper backing with the point. (Never score on the coated side because this tears off abrasive particles.) Then crease the abrasive material and tear it. Rip a cloth-backed paper over a sharp edge.

This abrasive pad looks like coarse felt. Actually it is a ¼-inch-thick pad of nylon fibers. They are coated with a very fine abrasive material. The pad is washable and used for wood finishing such as smoothing between coats of varnish. It also takes rust and corrosion from metals or fiber glass.

If you keep your abrasive materials clean, they work more efficiently for you. Clean coated abrasives by whisking off the excess material with a stiff brush. A metal-bristled filecard or a wire brush may be needed if the deposit is hard. When they are clean, the abrasive materials again work like new.

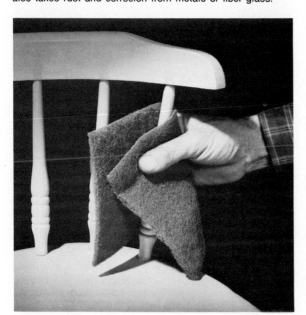

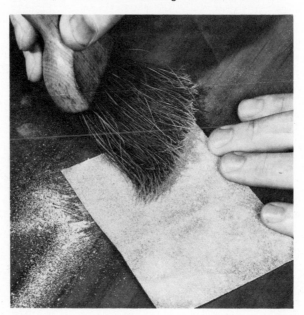

How To Select Decorations To Bring Your Rooms To Life

Rooms you remember longest, feel happiest in are those that reveal the tastes, the individuality of the people who live in them. Model rooms or furnished suites in hotels, however luxurious, are never indelibly imprinted upon your memory, because they are, in fact, anonymous—they reflect no one person's pattern of living.

There are no rules of thumb to guide the choice of "correct" accents and accessories, since your unique interests and taste must be primary influences. But it is possible to set forth some general principles that can help in selection and ways of displaying decorations so they will be in harmony with the setting you give them.

One could, perhaps, begin by considering *where* decorative objects may be placed to best effect. The largest available area in most rooms will, of course, be the walls. On them you can hang pictures, plaques, mirrors, maps, trays, dishes, and a variety of other fairly flat objects. By installing a shelf or series of shelves, it is possible to accommodate pieces having depth as well as height—such as the pieces of pewter, copper, and brass that form a part of the display across the page.

Useful objects decoratively displayed (kitchen utensils, old or new, large quantities of china or pottery tableware, and so on) are usually most appropriately used as wall decorations in kitchens and dining rooms; you can find tasteful examples of this kind of room accents and accessories in later pages of this section.

Floors, although they do not come first to mind, can also serve well as major areas available for the display of accent pieces, if these are in the form of area rugs or floor-based sculpture or large plants.

Windows, occasionally, can be fitted with glass shelves, and used as a display case for small plants or for collections of colored glass. Beware, however, of the temptation to show off too many things at the same time in such space, and risk an effect more cluttered than decorative. Learn to store part of your collection, give variety to the display by frequent changes.

In addition to such possible major areas for display as walls and floors, there are many spots in a room where one might put more functional decorative items such as screens, pillows, clocks, bowls and vases for flowers and fruit. Study rooms shown throughout this and succeeding volumes for new ways to use accent pieces artistically.

One wall of a dining area has been imaginatively equipped ▶ with shelves that act as shadow boxes for the display of a variety of beautiful, useful, amusing objects, as well as a number of prints and paintings. The collage effect obtained has appeal, and the items of which it is composed are in keeping with the overall provincial style of the room.

The fanciful pattern of the wall covering behind shelving is part of the picture. It is effective because most of the objects displayed against it are big enough to hold their own in competition with figured paper and are not, themselves, prominently patterned in ways that could conflict.

If you contemplate an assemblage of this kind, you will be wise to cut strips of paper to simulate shelves and to lay out your groupings on the floor first. In this way you can move things about, to check to see whether the balance is appealing before the wood is attached to the wall. *Then* suit spacing to whatever grouping of objects you find most aesthetic.

Selecting room accents requires imagination and inspiration. Occasionally, you will see an object and know it is right for some particular spot in your home. It is often instinctive knowledge that has led you to choose that piece over all of the other possibilities, and you may be unconscious of the factors that were involved in your intelligent selection.

If you are blessed with natural good taste, you will perhaps be satisfied with letting it operate for you without further concern for the principles that underlie an artistically wise choice. But most of us will benefit from going through a mental check list to give us more confidence in our ability to choose well.

The list will include such questions as: Is the style or period in harmony with the other furnishings? Is color suited to the basic color scheme? Is size in scale with other furnishings and with room location?

Most important of all, of course, is to decide whether or not you really like the particular item in question. If it doesn't please you in and of itself, don't choose it merely because it will "go with" your decorating scheme. Continue your search until you find the thing that both meets decorating needs and pleases your senses.

What you choose will, of course, depend upon your interests. If you are a collector of fine china cups or fishing flies, in all probability you'll want to display them. If you prefer one-of-a-kind pieces, each one of them could tell a little of the way you live and think.

Once the items are chosen, consider the way to display them most attractively. Do you want a symmetrical arrangement or an asymmetrical one? Will the objects be grouped or will they be shown singly. These are some of the basic facts you need to take into consideration.

This pair of pictures is well suited in color and style to the other room furnishings. The curves within the composition of the pictures offer pleasant contrast with the straight lines of furniture nearby. And they also offer the contrast of warm color against the cool green of the wall.

What is amiss is the way in which they have been hung. In a misguided attempt to secure variety, they have been hung in a staggered arrangement—one that is disturbing to the eye. Staggered pictures should follow architectural lines as when placing them against a staircase.

This pair of fruit pictures is now much more satisfying because they hang at the same height and so form a single visual unit, which balances the lamp's bulk. They are also hung at the eye level of an average person—another guide worth remembering when you are hanging pictures.

It is, of course, not possible to do this for all pictures if a sizable number are grouped; but in that event, you have hung them that way because you consider the grouping more interesting than any one item within it, and are not seriously concerned with whether the details of any one unit are seen.

We know at a glance that the person whose tastes and interests are reflected in the furnishings of this unusually decorated room is fascinated with the Napoleonic era. Since blue is a "receding" color, it was a wise choice for walls heavily decorated with colorful memorabilia of the "Little Corsican," such as gold epaulets mounted on red, pictures of the General framed in gilt, medals of the period, and so on.

One of the lessons we might learn from this display of a collector's treasures is that grouping small items on an appropriate background makes them more effective decoratively. Concentrating them in one area, rather than scattering them out over an entire room also heightens their appeal.

Another lesson to be learned from the handling of this room's decoration, focusing as it does on mementos of Napoleon, is that everything else in the furnishings—walls, floor covering, window treatment—is solid in color, simple in line.

The velvet drop curtain trimmed with gold cord is luxuriously appropriate to that period of his career when Napoleon was indeed "Emperor," but it does not steal attention from the main feature of the room—the collection.

Other than the objects that form this collection, the only ornate item in the room is the lamp fixture. But since this is hung above eye level, and is in keeping with the era, it does not detract from the fascinating things displayed.

Walls

Capitalize on walls as backgrounds for decorative accents. Make the most of the areas available by installing a series of shelves—built-ins or free-standing pieces of furniture especially made to serve as showcases for small treasures. The French have a word for this particular piece of furniture—étagère—and they vary its style to suit a room's other furnishings.

Ordinary bookcases, cabinets with glass doors, improvised shelving—any and all of these can serve your purpose, provided they are in harmony with other furnishings of the room in question.

Using all or most of a large wall in such a manner would make it the focal point of your decorating. Using a smaller amount of wall space this way could constitute an accent if not a major decorative feature.

For the next thirty pages, you will see examples of the tremendous variety of wall treatments whose most important goal is to lend decorative interest to a room.

The appropriate display of such elegant collectors' items as beautifully leather-bound books demands a vehicle as handsome in itself as this sophisticated shelving unit. The interesting curve of the tops is emphasized by the center placement in all three sections of wall-mounted plates of unusual design.

A collection of small boxes and chests, vases, goblets, bowls and the like occupies parts of some shelves along with books; it takes up other shelves entirely, for a pleasant variety.

Spotting a small high-intensity lamp upon a framed painting that rests upon a different shelf is an imaginative way of using space. This also breaks up any possible monotony that might result if the shelves were equally spaced.

Still another interesting variation is the manner in which one oblong painting, colorfully framed in red and black, has been fitted in to occupy an entire shelf unit.

Groupings as interesting as this one require experimentation on your part. Try out one arrangement, stand far enough off so that you see spatial relationships, and make alterations until you have balanced groupings and secured satisfactory variety.

Wall-hung shelving and the books, bottles, and other objects displayed upon them become the center of interest in one end of a room that has been furnished to serve as a comfortable study, with desk, chair, love seat, coffee table.

Although the approach to room decor has not been purist, the overall style is provincial. Mellow wood tones blend comfortably with the painted frame of the love seat and with the cheerful red and yellow color scheme that is dominant.

Other accessories in keeping with the traditional mood of furnishings include a lamp patterned after a three-branched candlestick, a bust of Napoleon, an antique box resembling a miniature desk, and a basket of china flowers.

An arrangement similar to this one might, with variations in style to suit your decorating preferences, be used in several rooms of most houses. The master bedroom is an excellent possibility. So is one corner of a kitchen-family room where the books might be cookbooks, with the desk and chair intended as the homemaker's office—the place where she compiles menus, pays bills, makes out shopping lists.

Or change the style again and have a grouping like this as a feature of a teen-ager's room. What better way to stimulate study periods than a comfortable setting? Books and accessories would be different in each case, depending upon the age and interests of the user, but the basic plan is adaptable.

If your home is so arranged that it includes any appreciable amount of wall space at the entry, plan to exploit it decoratively—as does this striking grouping of a painting, a candle sconce, a flower arrangement, and small sculpture.

Capitalizing upon the Spanish overtones of the strong ceiling beams of a family room beyond which can be seen, above the partial wall forming the entrance, decorative items displayed continue the Spanish theme. The small sculpture is, in fact, a "santo," (literally, a saintly person) and an example of a rapidly disappearing folk art now much sought after by collectors, and once common in the American southwest. In the same style is the candle sconce.

The red-green-yellow color scheme that appears in the entry decor is a continuation of colors used in the furnishings of rooms that can be seen in whole or in part as one enters the home. Rather unusual colors to combine, they continue the application of Spanish-Mexican modes to modern American home furnishings and decoration. In later volumes you will see examples of the currently stylish Mediterranean designs for home furnishings with which these accents would be compatible. Even if your preferred decorating style is entirely different from that pictured here, the plan for using wall space is one you may be able to adapt effectively in the choice of wall decorations. and other accents.

How to work wall magic

With paintings, with collections of art objects, with memorabilia and bibelots, or with useful objects—china, glassware, pottery, unusual cooking utensils—you can change a blank wall into an important center of interest, give a room the stamp of your own tastes, interests, personality.

To do this with authority takes imagination and awareness of what is appropriate in a given setting. Improve your ability to recognize what is suitable by asking a few pointed questions before you make final decisions on accents and accessories.

How to select well designed objects

Unless an object you intend to use as decorative accent is well designed, exclude it from even a place in a group of objects. To determine this, ask yourself these questions: Is it made in a craftsmanlike way? Are its lines graceful? If it is a complex object, are its parts in good proportion to each other? Well-illustrated books on whatever you are considering in the way of art or craft objects can help evaluate design. So can visits to art galleries and museums, especially to rooms furnished in styles of various periods.

In an unusual room, a tall stove made of faience (a type of ceramic) fulfills a major decorative role. Its importance is emphasized by a central position on a long wall, flanked by larger mural paintings of primitive style—a style that echoes the curiously antique style of the stove.

Other less important but interesting accessories take color cues from large floral-patterned fabric in which sofa and lounge chair are upholstered: yellow for lamp base and flowers; turquoise for domed dish on a coffee table. In an all-white room, dark touches of table tops, ceiling beams, exposed wood on sofa inject good contrast.

How to use compatible styles

If basic furnishings of the room in which you intend to place decorative pieces are all of one style, is the accent piece also of that style? If not, is it compatible?

This is not to say that mixes are out. Many are delightful. In fact, the eclectic is a most attractive style. Not suitable, as a rule, are combinations of formal and informal designs. For example, you would not hang a gilt-framed romantic picture of Marie Antoinette in a family room furnished in pine and chintz and expect a pleasing combination to result. The two styles would antagonize each other.

How to work with color and scale

Is the object or objects you intend using as wall decoration (or any other placement in the room) in scale with the other furnishings? If it looks too large or too small in relation to its surroundings it will not fulfill its decorative function.

Too, accent pieces need not match the basic room scheme, but they should be in harmony with it. A splash of color in the wrong place will destroy the effect of using color. The same holds true for accents. Harmony must be achieved in scale and color.

Black burlap supplies an inexpensive but dramatic background for a highly varied grouping of accessories. The rough texture of fabric and the color-absorbing quality of black allow an interplay of red, green, and gold accessories. Sizes and shapes vary widely, yet the grouping presents a unified visual picture that is a result of skillful placement.

The grouping works in this room because it is permitted to be the dominant decorating feature. You can dare to mix the different—old with new, functional with whimsical—if your goal is to be *avant garde,* and if you keep the rest of the room furnishings simple in line and pattern.

Notice that the fabric with which the contemporary sofa is upholstered is not one that demands attention—like the fabric used in the room across the page. The large coffee table and the things displayed upon it do not compete with the main center of interest—the objects displayed upon the wall. The floor covering is a solid color and contributes color and texture but not another distracting pattern to the whole.

◀ In a room as filled with interesting furnishings and decorative objects as this one, it is interesting to speculate on how it was possible to make a single painting clearly the focal point—and how you might achieve a similar result if you own a painting that you would like to be dominant in a room's decor.

First, the painting has been given a wall to itself—and this is an important clue to its importance in the scheme; second, it has been hung on a wall painted in a color closely related to the color most prominent in the picture itself; third, the nearest and largest piece of furniture—the sofa below—has been upholstered in an off-white, no-pattern fabric that 'repeats the color of the picture's matting.

Very different are the goals of the decorative use of walls in the room just above from the one across the page. In this invitingly casual and masculine setting, a display of a variety of sports trophies is the focus.

A series of built-in shelves, cupboards, drawers divides the wall space interestingly, and leaves open areas where trophies and pictures can be hung or set on shelves, with off-white and very dark brown as a background for the display.

For warmth, a wall of red, and the sofa, upholstered in striped fabric with red predominant, are wise choices. Note that the red is repeated on the opposite wall in the form of window shades. Tweedy neutral carpeting furthers the effectiveness of the injection of red as an accent color.

Simple, unadorned lines of the desk and chair, lamp and small table near the sofa are appropriate to the room scheme and do not take one's attention from the wall of trophies.

In a bedroom with ceilings somewhat lower than average, hinged panel screens covered in darkly dramatic fabric contrast sharply with walls of lighter value, and give an illusion of more height than is actually present.

Hanging a wall clock alongside the decorated window has reinforced the appearance of height, caused our eyes to travel upward from the level of nearby pieces of furniture.

Another ingenious and problem-solving treatment worth noticing is the handling of the window itself. Originally the height of its sill conflicted with the line of the desk in front of it. By using two shades—one raised from the bottom, the other lowered from the top—it was possible to hide sill line, and to create a backdrop for desk and chair.

Also interesting decoratively is the choice of a black desk chair, rather than one to match the wood of the desk itself. The dark tones within the fabric design are thereby echoed in a way that rather subtly helps the folding panels seem more related to other room elements. Also effective are a black rod on which panels are hung, and narrow bits of black trimming on both top and bottom edges of the window shades.

Echoing red tones within the patterned fabric are a red cushion for the rocking chair, and an accent rug that includes a variety of analogous shades of red, orange, and pink.

How to decorate for height

Of the major pieces of furniture used to equip our homes—chairs, tables, sofas, beds, desks, buffets—most reach no higher than midwall. If we did nothing to inject variety, through window treatments, wall-hung shelving, accents or accessories, the effect might be a monotonous all-one-height look, an imbalance of design as between the upper and lower halves of a room.

Although you may never have thought of it in this way, the commonest device for securing variety of height is through the use of draperies or other kinds of window treatment. Since windows do normally start at or near the ceiling line, it is necessary only to accent an architectural feature already present in order to get whatever emphasis on height you wish.

Another efficient way to secure the appearance of height is with decorative accents (pictures, groupings of ornamental objects, single tall mirrors) or, occasionally, with ceiling-hung light fixtures.

Here we present two examples of using decorative devices to carry the eye above the level of low pieces of furniture to secure a better balance between top and bottom halves of room designs. There are many other alternatives offered in the pages of this section on accessories and accents for walls. Study them for fresh ways to bring an appearance of height into any room where this would be of decorative value.

When a sizable sofa and the wall against which it is placed ▶ are of the same or almost the same color, decorative devices can be used to introduce an appearance of height, to draw the eye above the level of the sofa, and to avoid monotony.

For this grouping, the goal of height has been achieved by the placement of a wall grouping of decoratively framed mirrors, carved figures, and framed paintings. Supplementing the effect of height are wood strips with which the wool suede wall covering has been attached, as well as the group of three ceiling-hung light fixtures that are placed at the right of

To introduce variety into a basically monochromatic scheme, brightly colored pillows are piled on the sofa, and the floor is covered in striking black and white zebra stripes.

The tranquil mood pervasive in this living room stems from the natural look of fieldstone facing on a floor-to-ceiling fireplace wall, natural wood ceiling beams, and the neutral colors of the walls and the floor covering. For a dash of spice, chairs are covered in patterned fabric, and an imaginative grouping of pictures is placed on the wall at right of the fireplace. Picture placement is in good balance to tall stone wall.

Justifiably popular are the all-white walls and ceilings in homes where the display of paintings is to be a major decorative feature. In this case, colors from the abstract picture have determined the entire room scheme—blue of carpeting, brown of long, low wood bench, yellow and green accents of ottomans, pillows, flowers. For variety, a pillow on the far sofa is in a rosy hue that imitates minor colors used in the painting. White on sofas repeats white of walls.

How to copy a color scheme

If you own a painting whose theme and colors captivate you, use its appeal as the inspiration for the furnishings of the room in which it hangs. If it is totally modern in technique, it might lead you to choose furnishings and a color scheme such as those you saw a few pages earlier: White walls gave an appropriate background to a large abstract whose predominant blue and yellow hues influenced choice of upholstery fabrics and decorative accents.

How to capture a mood

If a painting of the group called genre pictures—of the kind that portrays everyday life (usually recognizable as Dutch, Spanish, Italian, and so on)—has a strong national feeling, it might inspire furnishing a room in the pure and vivid colors of, say, Mexico, and with pieces of furniture of the Spanish mission style.

You saw an example of this kind of influence in the entrance hall pictured some pages back, where a portrait of a woman set a Spanish theme for color and style.

A still life that features, primarily, fruits, wine, and objects related to the pleasures of the table is an eminently suitable choice to hang on a dining room wall.

In this case, the subject matter, the period (Nineteenth Century), and the colors have been echoed both obviously and subtly in the decorating scheme. A bowl of fruit that includes grapes looking just like those in the picture, a copper chafing dish of classic lines which repeats the metallic gleam of the pitcher in the painting—these are clear borrowings from the artist's composition. Because of the re-statement, the picture has become a far more important element of the room scheme than would otherwise have been the case.

Choice of other furnishings influenced by, rather than taken directly from, the painting include the old-fashioned clock—appropriate in period to the era evoked by the still life—and the checked tablecloth, as unpretentious in its way as are the things grouped by the artist.

The final influence of the painting upon the decor is evident in the color of the wall upon which it hangs. Its green is not identical to the greens within the painting, but is of a somewhat more intense but still harmonious shade that is flattering both to the picture and to the gilt of its antique frame, intentionally allowed to show signs of age.

"A blank wall means an empty eye," said a wise painter. He used this brief sentence to convey his philosophy concerning the world around us. But his viewpoint can be used to illustrate what can happen in decorating. Anyone who does not have some idea of color, motion, and composition will be satisfied with an expanse of plain walls.

Art pieces can fill that wall. They reflect personal habits, likes and dislikes. Most people are eager for the pleasures that attend choosing and hanging or mounting pictures and art objects in their homes.

Personal tastes have a wide range. Pictures of sorts can be bought at the supermarket or straight from an artist's easel—though originality is not necessarily synonymous with superior quality. Art objects may be bought at galleries or in a foreign country.

If the feeling that you lack the ability to choose wisely prevents you from acquiring original works of art—prints, paintings, sculpture—you can train your judgment. Read books and pamphlets from your public library, and study the articles and pictures in this encyclopedia.

For few pleasures are more intense or lasting than those accompanying graduation from the "I don't know anything about art, but I know what I like" stage to "this is why I like it." When you know why something is fine, sincere appreciation has replaced whim.

That is why living with art is like living with books—what you like to look at and what you like to read depend greatly on the experiences that have developed your taste.

However, keep in mind that appreciating art is a personal thing. Do not be misled into buying some piece of art you don't like because you are assured the piece is good. If it's not good for you to look at, then it is not good for you to buy. Buy for your family and for yourself. The art pieces on the walls should reflect your tastes.

Art is clearly a vital part of the lives of those who live here. There is a country feeling about this charming room, in which paintings blend harmoniously with discerningly selected antiques.

Wall colors are neutral in order to highlight pieces of art and Early Americana. Brick and vertical paneling painted white makes a handsome textured background. Rustic tartan plaid upholstery, and old pieces like the sled turned coffee table and the pewter weather-vane horse suit the country character of the house.

Sun colors for one section of a wall (opposite) have a visual ▶ effect of "advancing," and the use of them as background has heightened the importance of an arrangement of books and art objects as a major decorative feature of the room.

Bright blue bottles of various shapes, richly bound leather books, wood sculpture, paintings, and brass candlesticks have been given a dramatic background, arranged in an interesting asymmetrical design.

Select accessories; don't acquire them. If they're assets, their choice requires patience and discrimination.

If you feel you must gratify a relative or friend by displaying his gift, give it a bedroom placement unless it is something that will truly enhance the beauty of the rooms where guests will be received.

Don't be kind and put a gift painting on the mantel unless it's right there; store Aunt Emma's once fine teapot in a closet.

Brilliant scarlet-painted wall of wood paneling forms an ▶ exciting background for a grouping of abstract paintings. Not every kind of picture would be amenable to this sort of display. Realistic art, with a great deal of detail, would probably lose much of its appeal from competition with so bold a background. Here, the presence of lesser or greater amounts of red in each of the paintings, with their other hues predominantly black, white or gray, makes it possible for them to hold their own in this setting.

Notice that good overhead lighting has been supplied, which serves to light the pictures as well as the stairs. Even when pictures are hung where they receive excellent light in daytime hours, it is important to provide adequate artificial light for evenings—the time when family members and their guests will have most leisure to enjoy them.

A further decorative device was painting the classic grandfather clock that stands at the end of the hall in a red to match the walls—thus introducing very modern art.

There are ways to transform unimportant objects into decorations. The decoy duck below once swam in muddy waters. Battered and drab, it was rescued, varnished, waxed, given a new role as an ornament. The hunter is pleased and the duck looks decorative in compatible surroundings, accompanied by a pitcher of ivy and a polished pewter plate.

Sentiment has its place in determining what possessions we keep about us. But if an article to which we are sentimentally attached lacks artistic merit, we will be wise to place it in an inconspicuous spot. To display an object prominently is a tacit statement that we believe it to be of artistic merit and to have qualities that will enhance its surroundings.

Suitability is a major factor in choice of accents. What appeals to us in a gallery or shop may take on an entirely different character in our living room. That's because the background and atmosphere are not the same.

The abstract that looked dramatic in the gallery may seem out of place at home. Avoid a costly mistake. Before investing in any major purchase try it out at home. "Little things," in judging decorating schemes as in judging persons, are important. They can make or mar a person or a room.

In planning the furnishings of our home, we may hesitate to add the "little things" that could make all the difference between a home with individuality or one merely utilitarian. It is wise to test out our impulses concerning the suitability of an object in its projected placement, but it is important to put something of ourselves into the furnishings of our homes, both to satisfy our inner needs for beauty, and to tell others in ways that speak clearer than words about our values and tastes. Be selective, but do put yourself in the scheme.

A large expanse of wall is a perfect background for a grouping of pictures like the one below. The neutral bricks need some decoration, and their textured surface gives off a pleasing gallery look to a private collection.

Large pictures are hung at eye level; smaller ones placed in satisfying balance. No one picture overpowers another. When building or remodeling, plan for a display such as this.

Single paintings can be dramatic accents when they are used as a focal interest in a room. Exciting colors win the painting, above, its solo placement. There is nothing timid or so-so about that great red circle, and guests may sit before the fire speculating happily about the swirl and skid of colors and the possible intention of the artist. Some rooms require a single gesture—such as this one—to bring them to life.

Enjoyment of art tells others something about you. It is the wise purchaser who prepares himself with in-depth knowledge of styles, mediums, techniques, and composition before he makes a major investment. A safe test of whether a painting will have long-lasting appeal for you is to see whether you are drawn back after your first sight of it.

There is a country feel to the room below, and it has an expectancy about it. You believe that the people who live here are friendly and relaxed. Natural woods, mellow colors, Early American furniture have much to do with establishing the mood. There is nothing forced about it, and the entire effect is one of cheerfulness that invites companionship.

The neutral wall is a logical background for American primitive paintings: a duck a-bob on blue-green water; sun-flowers blooming freely; a tree slicing through bright canvas.

Accessories should contribute to a sense of "wholeness," or an all-of-a-piece coordination. That is exactly the impression left by the room below. It is true some rooms need shock treatment such as the bold canvas opposite. But in that case the entire room was made subordinate to the large painting.

Here, the appeal of a variety of things is the key. In a country kitchen and family-dining room, a table built around a post, curving brass candlesticks and copper match holder to decorate the post all blend harmoniously with overall style.

The right frame makes a tremendous difference in the appeal of a painting. A well-chosen frame is, first, suited to the work of art itself—both in size and style; secondly, it takes into account the setting in which it is to be hung.

In general, the larger the picture, the wider or more prominent the frame you will choose to obtain proportion, though there are times when a heavier than average frame is flattering to a small picture—especially if it is in an older style or truly an antique.

Except for prints, lithographs, and similar works of art which are all black and white themselves, a black frame is not a good choice. Frames of natural wood, pale tints, gilt or silver will better focus attention on the work of art, not the frame.

Some wall-mounted works of art require no frames, as is true of these three bronze plaques, although they could have been mounted if that technique had been preferred. To keep them shining without the need of frequent polishing, they have been sprayed with a coat of protective lacquer.

Many modern sculptors produce works that are intended for wall mounting rather than display on a stand—as would be true for any piece having three dimensions, meant to be seen from all sides. Such pieces are most effective as decorations when they are given a special background, preferably of rough texture, if their gleam is a vital part of their appeal. This background can be supplied inexpensively with floor-to-ceiling strips of burlap in neutral colors or colors tied into those that are predominant in other furnishings of the room.

If your goal is to compose a design by grouping a number of prints or sketches (or, as in this case, a number of favorite recipes) you may find narrow black frames a suitable choice for the purpose. This technique assumes that the pattern formed by grouping is visually more interesting than the content of any one of the items within the group that is so framed.

In a wall grouping that includes pieces of china and porcelain ▶ as well as a cherub figure and reproductions of interesting designs once used at the top of columns, a wide variety of framing has been used for the pictures that make up the bulk of the assemblage. Just because there is such a wide variety of items included in the group—things which bear no relation to each other in style or color—the variety of framing styles seems appropriate. Were there more similarity within the total, greater similarity of style would have been better.

Grouping objects and pictures as diverse as these in a pleasing arrangement takes careful planning. Test out your groupings before you begin to drive nails by laying them out on an open floor space in the same approximate relation they will have on the wall. Shift items until you achieve a good balanced composition.

Overall harmony is a constant goal when we add accessory and accent pieces to the furnishings of a room. It is relatively easy to secure when both furniture and accents are of the same period.

More difficult, but usually far more interesting, is the harmony that results when we combine basics and accents of different styles and periods, harmonious because of pleasing not warring contrasts. Pleasing contrasts are those that set an ornate against an unornamented design, dark against light, smooth against rough, shiny against dull. Each element is more appealing because of the contrast than if it were surrounded by other items like itself.

Before you choose accessories and accents, examine the basic furnishings of a room to see which kinds of contrasts you most need to enhance the appeal of what you have.

In an entrance hall with floor of plain quarried tile and white walls, we can indulge in—and enjoy—the introduction of patterned contrast. We have it here in baroque picture framing and fancifully carved hall bench. Also strongly patterned, but more geometrical, is a small rug of oriental design. Continuing the ornate theme is an umbrella stand of highly polished brass with handles in classic design.

Returning to the simple lines of the basic architecture is a simple, oval tub which serves as a cachepot for a large, shiny-leaved rubber plant (a good growing choice for a hall where light is not strong). Cushion on bench is solid in color, but patterned by its tufting, and so better related to the bench than a plain cushion would have been. The total effect is one of harmony gained through contrast and repetition.

Groups of objects as decorations are most effective when they are related to one another in one or more ways—color, material of which they are made, style, period. If the relationship is obscure, the eye is apt to rove restlessly over the grouping in order to discover why they're placed together. When you are planning a wall decoration of this sort, make sure there is a visible link that unites the separate elements.

Plan for changes of scene in the smaller pieces that make up the accessories and accents of the rooms of your home. Orientals have long had storerooms called "godowns" for the safekeeping of scrolls, vases, china ornaments, and so on, when they are not on display. Seasonal or more frequent changes of such decorations can be made regularly. This is one of the best ways that you can keep your wall looking vibrant, alive year round.

Generally, accessories are the final touch that adds a rich spark of personality to a room. But this is not always the case, as with the informal dining room below. Here, an entire room was planned around a collection of Meissen ware. The blue and white color scheme and the pattern for the ceiling-high stenciled border were borrowed from the German porcelain collection. But having the proper color scheme and accessories is only part of the design story. Without a working arrangement, accessories add only clutter, not interest, to a room. Creating a focal point as well as attractively displaying the varied pieces of porcelain, the narrow shelf stretching across the wall establishes an atmosphere of Old World charm perfect for informal entertaining. It is accessorizing at its best.

There is a natural affinity between much of the most modern of furnishings and primitive art forms. The two here are combined to good effect. Muted colors of wall, floor covering, and fabric in which the sofa is upholstered are appetizingly spiced with jewel tones of pillows, flowers, decorative box on the white pedestal-style table—the colors constituting a subtle reminder of the primitive style of pieces on the wall.

Time was—and not too long ago—when the vogue of "functionalism" turned kitchens into rooms that bore rather close resemblance to hospital operating rooms. Lost in that shuffle were hominess, warmth, the age-old inviting character of the heart of the home—the place where food's prepared.

All that has changed with the discovery that there is no basic incompatibility between the friendliness of brick and wood and the efficiency of modern appliances. A mechanical dishwasher works quite as well when it's installed behind a panel of pine. Ranges are quite as effective in kitchens papered in chintz, floored with brick as in laboratory-sterile settings.

Useful items decoratively displayed are once more in fashion in kitchens that invite family and friends to gather 'round, and to share in the conviviality that can attend the preparation of the meal. Collections of pewter, pottery, arrays of gleaming copper vessels, jars of dried herbs and spices, bowls and baskets of fruit, strings of red peppers or purple onions—all these are decorations to make kitchens happy places.

The kitchen pictured here aptly illustrates the points we've just been discussing—that useful items, decoratively displayed, make today's kitchens among the most inviting of rooms.

Rough, exposed ceiling beams and an open fireplace look like those our founding fathers once favored. They have a friendly, unpretentious character that suggests you'll enjoy the time spent in this room, as cook or as family members who gather here at night to share good talk while enjoying the look and smells of good food being prepared for an evening meal.

In character with the mood established by ceiling beams and fireplace are the displays of pewter and glass that decorate the wall space between windows and the mantel above the fireplace. Also in the mood is the interesting antique light fixture and the pewter tea and coffee service on the counter top.

Appliances are entirely modern, but are cleverly hidden behind old chestnut paneling; they include a refrigerator, ice-maker, dishwasher, and warming oven. Electric burners set into the countertop near the sink are contemporary but offer no conflict with the Early American styling of the room and of the antique pieces that serve to decorate it.

Half a lamp was better than a whole one for this small bedside cabinet. With considerable ingenuity, these home-owners had a brass base and the shade cut in two, mounted against the wall. The other half is placed on the matching stand at the other side of the double bed. When selecting bedside lamps, check that its light will be cast down on book.

Arrange useful objects needed for bedside comfort in a grouping that will add to your overall decorating scheme.

Lamps, ashtrays, alarm clocks, telephones, books—these are some of the things you may want close at hand. They can be decorative assets if they are attractively grouped and suited in scale and color to the rest of a decorating scheme. Scale, especially, will be a factor worth careful consideration, for nothing is less attractive than a number of sizable objects piled on a small tabletop—one the size of a usual bedside table.

Besides scale and color, you should consider whether objects are of a style or design compatible with the furnishings as a whole, and especially with the objects they'll be grouped with. If everything else is formal, don't spoil the effect by introducing an accessory of "op art" or "mod" design. Save it for a more appropriate setting.

Banish bedside clutter by storing small comforts—paper tissues, cough drops, reading glasses, or what you will—inside doors or drawers of a bedside table.

If no doors or drawers for storage exist, search out a handsome box that will be a decorative asset, and place it on your bedside table. Or set a small chest like the one shown at right beneath your table. There's room, too, for a cushion to prop you up when reading in bed.

A good rule to follow when deciding how many accessories you'll place on view on a table top is to make sure one-third to one-half of the space is left empty. Nothing's better than a little clear background to make the remaining accent and accessory pieces show off to best advantage.

For most tastes, this lamp is too large to suit its placement on a bedside table. One of about two-thirds its size would have been in better scale. And if the occupant of the twin bed at left likes to read in bed, the location would be unsatisfactory. For such purposes one of the lamps that has a single base but two directional lamps would have been a better choice.

Shelves are versatile helpers when you want to get maximum storage from a minimum amount of wall space, and secure some decorative benefits as well.

The variety possible is really infinite, since they may be built of many woods as well as man-made materials, painted or finished to suit the room, spaced at intervals to accommodate the size of objects you want to store on them. Even the readymade shelving offers a large choice of styles, sizes, and finishes to meet your special needs.

The creative part comes in when you plan how to arrange the objects you'll store on open shelves. Arrange them for convenience, if they're things you need to use frequently; place seldom-used objects on the higher, harder to reach shelves.

Next, if the total effect is to be attractive, you should experiment with several ways of grouping the items so as to get variety, balance, and a pleasant overall effect from the assemblage. Check your arrangement for balance and design by standing far enough back so you see it as a unit.

When convenience and a balanced arrangement have been secured in your grouping, see whether colors are right in relation to the rest of the room's furnishings. If the total is a bit drab, get color the easy way with bright paper jackets for books, paint for some items—or for the shelves themselves—or a framed print with colorful mat.

In a small bedroom—and they are the rule rather than the exception in modern homes—a shelf arrangement like this one is both convenient for storage, and attractive to look at.

Wall standards and brackets of this kind are available in hardware stores. They come in a variety of finishes such as brass, copper or silver, even in gunmetal and black. Wall brackets are in matching finishes with ready-made shelving of either pine or redwood. Or make your own shelves and finish to coordinate with colors of your room scheme.

You can complete the installation of a group of shelves like this in about two hours. Drop plumbline and mark strategic points. Drill holes, tap plastic anchors in; screw standards to the wall. Brackets fit into standards and shelves rest on top. Lower shelves are 12 inches deep; others are nine inches.

Brick walls are almost always congenial backgrounds for the display of accessories. Their rough texture, mellow earth tones flatter many kinds of accent pieces.

A two-shelf arrangement that runs the length of a wall offers space for books, small accessories below, larger, bolder pieces above, and also gives meaning to the wall display above shelves of paintings and a variety of decorative accessories. Notice how balance and variety have been secured through grouping.

A foyer wall, below, serves as a display area for an interesting and varied collection of paintings, plaques, and sculptures, and an unusual hand-carved mirror frame resembling many small and somewhat irregular circles of wood.

By hanging pictures and other ornamental objects all the way to the ceiling, a visual raising of the ceiling's height has been accomplished—something worth remembering if your home has ceilings lower than you like.

How to use shelves to unify groupings

Shelves unify groupings of accessories given wall placement. Capitalize on this when you have ornamental pieces of various kinds that are interesting in themselves but are not large or impressive enough to justify single placement.

The shelf treatment is extremely flexible, adaptable to almost any setting. On these two pages you see shelves serving as frames or display cases for accessories appropriate to a dining room, kitchen, entry hall, and living room. Vary shelf style to suit room placement and the character of decorative pieces it will display.

Plan well in advance for spacing appropriate to the size and height of accents to be placed on shelves for display.

In the dining room pictured below, small space is handled with flair. A pair of *étagères* (French name for open-shelf pieces of this sort) flank the window, fitting neatly into space too small to accommodate a buffet. On their shelves are ranged a display of decorative pieces related to dining.

A focal point is an artistic necessity not only for paintings but for overall decorating schemes. If a room lacks any center of interest that instantly captures your attention on entering, it has failed from a decorative viewpoint.

One of the ways to give a room focus is through capitalizing upon wall space with a shelf or series of shelves holding interesting objects and collections that lend *cachet* to the whole. (*Cachet* is a French expression meaning a very personal stamp that sets a room apart from the ordinary.)

Depending upon what you wish to display, you'll have narrow or wide shelves, shelves widely spaced or close together. If you're the least bit of a handyman, you can build your own to suit exactly the space available, finish them to harmonize with colors in the particular room scheme.

Narrow shelves require careful handling because they limit the ways you may group accessories. Some things, if they're very much alike—collections of china cups, for example—may take nicely to being arranged all in a line. But you'll still be wise to leave ample space between items. Resist an urge common to collectors to put all of a collection on view at once. Don't do it if you want others to see the beauty of and to share your enthusiasm for each piece.

On wide shelves, try out various ways of grouping the objects you want to display. Try for variations of shape and height so that the resulting contrast enhances your overall effect. Stand well back and check to see whether the grouping does have both balance and variety. If not, regroup and re-examine the result.

If the pieces to be displayed are not very colorful in themselves, consider painting the shelves to increase the attention-getting quality of the grouping. Choose shelf color that is harmoniously related to other colors in your furnishing scheme.

Display shelves you can make and hang in two hours decorate a kitchen or family-room wall. Almost any wood will do for these—hardwood or just pine boards. Make two 1 × 1-inch uprights a couple of feet long and drill a series of holes along inside edges to receive wire hangers.

Fasten uprights that are to support the series of shelves to the wall with screws or toggle bolts. Cut shelves from 1 × 4-inch and 1 × 8-inch boards. Bend hangers from coat hangers or clothesline wire. To hook in holes underneath shelves, go around and hook just above. Stain or finish to suit the wall and other room furnishings.

The joys of cooking can be expressed no more aptly than by the decorative display of useful objects employed in preparing food. Today's handsomely designed pots and pans, casseroles, storage jars, knives, long-handled forks and spoons deserve better than to be hidden away in cupboards.

European chefs have shown us that honest shapes and shining finishes of utensils that are used in cooking are the best of all possible decorations for the room where meals are prepared. They are both suitable and highly decorative, if well displayed.

Wall racks are one of the best means of turning kitchen utensils into decorations. They keep the useful items handy for use, out of the way when not needed, and readily visible as part of the room scheme.

Color possibilities are almost endless, for today's cooking wares come not only in copper, aluminum, stainless steel and other shining metals, but in enamel finishes of almost every hue imaginable—bright blues, oranges, reds, avocado green, buttercup yellow, as well as white with colored trims. If your kitchen is drab, see what you can do decoratively with everyday useful objects.

It is obvious at a glance that this is a modern kitchen that includes every useful appliance, and it is well arranged for efficiency; but its design has not stopped there.

The entire area has an appealing decorator look due to the accessories that are both utilitarian and ornamental. Wall-hung copper pots and pans, glassware visible behind glass cabinet doors, collectors' items displayed atop cabinets, a chandelier-style light fixture that pleases because it dares to be different—these are some of the accessories that give character, beauty, eye-filling variety to what might have been just another very modern, well-equipped kitchen.

There is a basic lesson to be learned from this kitchen: if you plan to display a wide variety of items related to food and cooking as room decoration, keep the color scheme and the background simple. Here, blue and white and the brown wood tones of the cabinets furnish an excellent background that focuses attention on accessories, and avoids the danger of a cluttered look that can result if multiple objects are displayed against a background that is, itself, an attention-getter.

Rugs

Area rugs are less than room-size carpets that knit furniture groupings together. They come in various shapes, sizes, textures, and designs, and can be used in many ways. Not to be confused with scatter rugs, they can be used over your wall-to-wall carpeting as attention-getters, as dirt catchers in heavily traveled areas, and can be hung on the wall where you need imaginative, textured ideas. Accent rugs are smaller than area rugs and are used to add color or interest to your floor.

Formerly, rugs or carpets were judged by their weaves. Now they are woven, tufted and knitted, and are made with man-made fibers as well as wool or cotton.

Acrylics, rayons, nylons, and polypropylene are examples of man-made fibers. They are mothproof, mildew resistant, maintain good color quality, and generally are inexpensive. But like all fabrics, they need care and attention.

Man-made fiber rugs and carpets should be cleaned carefully—vacuumed lightly each day and thoroughly each week. An absorbent powder, also, should be applied twice a year to help bring up the color; and once every few years the rug or carpet should be professionally cleaned.

Where to use them

Area rugs can fit in any room in your house: hallway, bedroom, kitchen, living room, dining room, and family room. They are almost indispensable in the front hall, especially in wet weather.

There, rugs are not doormats but serve as handsome hall decorations. Choose one that picks up the dominant hall color but stands on its own. If your carpeting or floor is plain, select one that has a bold pattern. Solid-colored rugs fit best in a hallway with figured carpeting or bright and busy tile.

Do the same in all other rooms in your home. But while the color scheme is a major determinant in your choice of area rug, do not forget quality and life, too. In areas that take a lot of traffic—hallways, bedrooms, kitchens— decide on a rug that will take hard work, and that will not break down easily when washed. Cotton or synthetic-fiber rugs are best. And frequently a more expensive rug is worth the additional cost. A dense pile for the hall, for example, will be more expensive, but you profit from your initial investment in time saved cleaning up the carpeting or wiping up the tile.

There are many uses to which you can put area or accent rugs. Only your imaginativeness sets the guide-lines. In living rooms they provide accent either on the floor or the wall. By using a rug with vivid colors, you can turn a smooth-surfaced wall into a center of interest. And one can deaden the noise in a much traveled room. Area rugs can also act as partitions, to set off a sleeping area from a study in a combination room or to hold an eating area together in the kitchen.

In the next few pages, we will show how these rugs serve to draw all the elements of a room together—pulling curtains, pictures, furniture into the central color and decorating scheme.

Where to use area rugs

Area rugs that draw together conversational furniture groupings should be large enough to outline the groups. Each piece of furniture should be set at least partially on the rug. For example, an area rug that you place in front of a sofa should be as long as the sofa or longer.

Each furniture group should fit comfortably on the rug. If not, it will resemble a placemat that is too small to hold all the glasses and silverware.

Notice how a shaggy, looped-pile rug keeps the living-room furniture together. It holds the chairs and settee in a conversational grouping and sets off the dining area from the rest of the room. This division is further emphasized by having the same color in the rug and in the furniture. This color is also restated in the draperies. All other elements of the room harmonize. The black square table sitting on a square rug ties in with the black chairs. And the two colors used in the chair seats harmonize with other colors in the room. What you have is a room that is divided.

Imagine leaping out of bed and onto this deep shag rug. Not only does it supply comfort underfoot, but it provides the largest area of color in the room. This rug extends the length of the bed, and draws in the table and stools. And the texture of the rug provides a welcome contrast to all other surfaces.

The record player next to the twin bed sets the mood for a daytime retreat for playing music if you have no guests.

Actually this is a room of many colors united by neutrals. Blue is the dominant color, and it ties the room together. It is found in the rug, and is picked up by the wall hanging and the occasional pillow. The black spread and white walls provide tasteful contrast.

Accent colors can be bright when used in combination with black and blue. A clever use of reds and yellows in the chairs and pillows perks up the scheme.

The window treatment is simple but works well with the other colors and shapes. It emphasizes the line of the wall hanging and repeats its color in the shades. And the white woodwork carries the vertical white stripes around the corner.

Avoid contrasting colors

It is difficult to use two colors in the same room unless the room is large, or you choose colors that contain a common family hue such as orange and yellow-orange. Even when using two related colors, they also should be close in value and intensity.

Combining different colors is easiest in a combination living-dining room. The colors must still be related, but each room can be given a different color emphasis. If the colors in both rooms are green, gold, and wood tones, select green as the color for the area rug in one room and gold for the other room. The same wood tones would carry over in both rooms. And the accent color would alternate, too. In this way your rooms would balance, yet color will define each functional area.

Select rugs for shape

Rugs come in different shapes and sizes. Select that shape which best fits your furniture. Do not marry a square rug with a round table. And settle on one that is larger than the area. A good rule of thumb is to buy a rectangular rug. This shape can be moved from area to area and will generally suit the mood.

How to choose a bedroom rug

A bedside rug, which should be as long as the bed, is used to provide a comfortable warm spot on which to slip from your bed. But it can also be used to section off a room, if you have a combination bedroom-study, and to outline a table, a lamp and a couple of chairs to provide a small sitting space.

Again, it can act as the focal point for your decorating scheme. Many rugs are available in various colors to set a balance between your furniture style and the color scheme.

And, as bedroom rugs do not get the heavy wear that hall or living-room rugs do, this is one time when you can save a little on the quality of rug that you buy.

Matching Moroccan area rugs, aglow with vibrant color and geometric patterns, form an almost wall-to-wall carpeting look. The jewel tones of the rugs seem to emphasize the natural beauty of polished wood floors.

The rugs separate two conversational groupings in this large living room. They also are allowed to dominate other colors in the room. Walls, draperies, and upholstered pieces are purposely cooled by quiet white, which brings out the warm rug tones. The charcoal chair and dark woods seem to

be inspired by colors in the rug, too. The sharpest accent color is yellow, which is seen in the brass accessories and lamp base. Even the colors of the books in the white bookshelves seem to repeat those in the magnificent rugs.

Think how these rugs would look if they were placed kitty-corner to the walls. They would disrupt the whole room. Instead of order, you would have disorder. It is important to note that area rugs should be placed so that they follow the structural lines of the room.

A large, golden-brown area rug is the dominant feature in this generously sized room. Not only does it provide the central color scheme, it also helps to establish room size. If the furniture were placed against the walls of the room, guests might have to shout at one another to make themselves heard. Rather than break the space up into conversational groupings, this rug was selected to bring the furniture in from the walls. Now traffic can flow around the outside of the room, leaving the middle free.

Without the rich rug tones, the large expanses of white would make the room look sterile. A lighter, but still clear, gold in the sofa picks up the central color and conveys it to the picture on the wall. This is repeated in the dark, wealthy tones in the bookcase.

This feeling of confluence is further emphasized by the oval glass tables. Each table helps to draw the two areas together for a unified appearance.

Here's a rug that you can make. Strips of various sizes, shapes, and colors are sewn over a solid felt base. Closely related colors, without too much contrast, work best. Before you sew the pieces down, pin them to the felt so you can try different arrangements. It's not difficult to create a pattern, but it is important that you achieve a pleasant composition.

When you find the arrangement that you feel is right, baste the pieces to the felt. Your material won't wrinkle if you sew every seam in the same direction. Top-stitch fringe around the rug and you won't have to bother with hems.

The example shown here provides a brilliant color contrast to other neutral furnishings. The brown fringe picks up other colors in the room. The rug is made long enough to fit in front of the fireplace and is wider than the chairs.

How to select rugs for bath and kitchen

Wherever you're likely to run into spots and spills, it's best to think about washable fabrics. No matter how careful you are, someone is going to upset a cup of coffee or glass of milk. Fortunately, there are many kinds of rug materials in a wide range of colors that will fill the bill. Cotton and synthetic fibers, including indoor-outdoor carpeting, can be used fearlessly. As an area or accent rug, one can be an island of color which holds an eating area together, or it can give protection from spills at the sink—especially when children help with the washing up.

In the bathroom, even with wall-to-wall carpeting, you still need a bathmat or an area rug before the wash basin. Cut a free-form shape that suits your bathroom's dimensions and sew tassels, fringe, or braid on it. Then use the same material to trim curtains.

How to use fur area rugs

Fur area rugs, either real or imitation (since imitations now look genuine), are the ultimate in luxury. They add real glamour to most rooms. Since these accent rugs are usually small, you have to place them where they'll be in scale with their surroundings. Such good rugs require special attention. Real furs need a rest in a cool place in hot months. Imitations can be washed gently and brushed when dry.

◄ A fur area rug claims the center of attention in this contemporary room. Its soft, deep pile contrasts superbly with other hard and shiny surfaces. Its length is the same as the sofa's, so it holds this comfortable conversation area together. It also provides pattern in the room, yet does not argue with the graceful shapes in the wallpaper. These are similar in scale and tied together by their black color.

Notice also the pleasant blend of shapes and colors in this sophisticated room. The swirling lines of the fur and the wallpaper are complemented by the round shapes of the table, chairs, and lamp base. Structural lines and other heavy shapes, like the sofa near the wall, are squares. The dominant colors are black, white, and wood tones. These colors would seem drab if it were not for the ripe reds in the fabric on the sofa and in the wallpaper. Pattern here provides transitional lines between shapes and ties important colors together. The clever combination of shape and color makes sharp contrasts pleasing to the eye.

This area rug has important fringe benefits. It is cut from a piece of indoor-outdoor carpeting. The edges are rounded to copy the shape of the table, since a square rug here would appear awkward. The fringe was glued around the edges with fabric cement. It adds color as well as texture to the grouping.

Indoor-outdoor carpeting is available in 3-6-9-12-foot widths. It's made from a synthetic, non-woven fiber that resists stains, fading, and moisture. For the rug shown here, a 6 × 9-foot piece of fabric was used, and the carpet area measured to allow room for chairs to slide back without disturbing the fringe.

How to care for area rugs

A rug's fiber determines the standard for its care. Wool rugs need more specialized attention than cotton or synthetic rugs.

Vacuuming wool rugs frequently removes loose soil. You can clean up spots with soap and water. Before the rug gets too dirty, send it to a professional cleaner.

Cotton and synthetic fibers can usually be machine washed and dried, according to the instructions that accompany your rug. Rugs with a plushy pile should be brushed when barely dry.

Indoor-outdoor rugs can be sponged off with soap and water. Spots wipe up easily.

How to choose an area rug

Before you start shopping, measure the area you want to cover. By studying the placement of furniture you already have, you can see how you can rearrange it to use a rug to better effect. Although you can buy area rugs in many sizes, some are more common than others. Choose one that's a little larger than you need rather than one much smaller. Most rugs are rectangular in shape, but you can get round, hexagonal or free-form ones. You can decide which shape is best for you by studying other shapes in your room.

The color you choose for your area rug should help your color scheme, not conflict. If you have trouble finding just the color you want, consider a blend of several colors that will harmonize with those you have in your room. To unite the scheme, you can use the other colors in the rug for accessories or accents.

How to use designer's rugs

These are most costly. They are often one of a kind and may have the designer's name on the back. They could be the kind you'll want to use as a wall hanging. Some have hand "carving," which increases cost and beauty.

◄ What was once a bare attic has been transformed into a colorful guest bedroom by an imaginative use of color and pattern. Each complements the other.

Startlingly bold, a dramatic area rug catches the eye and sets the theme. The yellow in the rug is picked up and splashed about the room: in the pillows on the bed, the lamp shades, the flowers on the clever corner-shelf, and in the giant napkins lying on the tea table.

Equally as strong, though muted in intensity, the brown tones of the rug are repeated in the wall-to-wall carpet, the table, the chest, the wicker basket at the foot of the bed, and in the bed coverlet. The effect is one of harmony.

Harmony is present, too, in the patterns in this room. The geometric shapes in the area rug come from the same family as those seen in the wallpaper. This pattern is picked up and carried over into the large, fringed pillows serving as part of the headboard and in the cushions on the chairs.

To offset the vivid colors, the designer injected white into the color scheme. Dotted about the room in the chairs, the wallpaper, shelving, and in the rafters, this non-color serves to highlight the two dominant colors.

An area rug is meant to define an area. Here the rug only outlines tables. Two small tables have been crowded together to fit in the middle of a rug that serves no real decorative function. The color itself is not wrong; it blends well with the green and wood tones in the room. But the rug fails to draw together the sofa and tables.

The fault here is that the rug is too small to bring the tables and sofa into the right proportion. Also, it will get in the way as you walk between the sofa and the tables. If you have any doubts about size when you shop, it is safer to choose the larger of two sizes.

This area rug carries out its function by including all the pieces of furniture within its borders. Now it's possible to divide the cube tables to create a more spacious look. If you compare the two pictures, the sofa appears longer when the rug is larger.

The choice of a patterned rug for this area was wise, for it breaks up an expanse of solid colors. The rug's design generates interest in the grouping and yet is in good scale with the size of the tables and other furnishings. It is a good example of how a little pattern can make a setting appear richer in detail. It's detail that makes the difference.

The artist who designed this area rug used wools instead of oils as his medium. The vibrant colors show the planning of someone who knew how to keep the eye moving—one of the prerequisites for a good painting. Sea blue mingles with yellow, pink, orange, and green. Finally the blue dies out—lost in a crescendo of red, pink, and orange. The cool colors have been defeated by the warm family. Does it seem to be trying to tell you something? Let your imagination go free. Maybe you will discover a blue ocean being swallowed up by the brilliance of a sunset. Maybe you'll see something different in its whirling colors. That's part of the beauty of an abstract design. You find your own action in it.

1/4"plywood 3/4"plywood

area·rug

If a rug is pretty enough to have come from an art gallery, it may seem a shame to let people walk on it. Here's one solution—hang it on your wall. Maybe you'd like to go a step further and treat it like a painting by framing it.

The dimensions of this rug are 4 × 6 feet. It is framed with 6-foot-long boards, stained dark. Quarter-inch plywood is set far enough back into the boards to make the rug flush. The back is held together by ¾-inch plywood strips.

This rug was hung on a stairway landing that could use more light. Fluorescent tubes were placed at the top and bottom of the frame to reflect light up and down. The sketch above explains the construction of the inner frame and placement of the tubes.

You can adjust these measurements to fit any size rug. To hang the frame, drill holes in the back boards and screw the unit to the wall. Some accent rugs are quite heavy. You may need more than just a couple of screws. Use them at the top and bottom of the frame. The cost for framing will be just a few dollars. The price of the whole unit will depend upon the cost of the rug.

You can use this same framing idea to hang fabrics wherever you need decoration and light. Or, frame a collection of objects, such as a bunch of artificial flowers or a group of old pocket watches.

Plain or patterned?

It depends primarily on your floor. You'll find that a bold-patterned rug on a bold patterned floor is not a happy combination. For instance, if your floor happens to be a checkerboard tile or a lovely pegged oak, a solid color will do most for you. But an intricately pat-

terned rug will look best with relatively plain walls and plain furniture.

Is padding necessary?

Not always, because some area rugs have a latex coating on the back. Others have an attached layer of foam. Either of these backings will keep the rug in place and prevent it from skidding. There is also a liquid latex product that you can brush on the back of your rug if it doesn't have a backing. You can use the same material to renew a latex coating that has worn off through repeated washings and years of wear.

Many rugs are so thick that you won't need a pad. In fact, if you try to use padding under them, you'll find yourself—and your guests—tripping on them. However, padding will make a thin rug feel more luxurious.

If you choose to put padding underneath, there are several varieties. Foam rubber padding is made in a couple of thicknesses. Select the one that feels best under your foot but doesn't stick up too high. Felt pads are thinner and less expensive.

Shopping tips for rug buyers

If you're looking for a quality rug, watch for those that have a dense pile. They're more expensive but they'll wear longer. For this reason, it is best to buy a good grade for living rooms or hallways that get lots of wear. You can buy a lesser quality for rooms that are out of the traffic pattern. For a few dollars, you can get both good style and color.

Both natural and synthetic fibers are good buys dollar-wise. But you don't have to judge a rug on fiber content alone. Your best values in the long run are known brands. Look for the label with the recognizable manufacturer's name. It will tell you the fiber content, pattern, and color name. If the rug is washable, the tag will tell you how to do it—what kind of soap to use, the temperature of the water, and if the rug can be tumble dried.

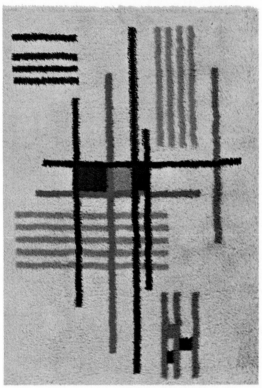

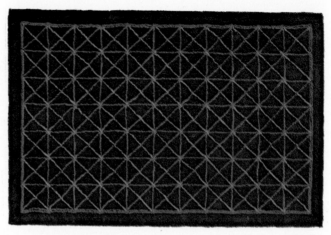

Overstitched loops of bright color play against an unusual deep-hued Acrilan high plus background in *Party Time*. This particular area rug is available in six vibrant color combinations to suit a variety of color schemes, and in several sizes as well.

This modern adaptation of an Aubusson tapestry motif makes an elegant foil for furniture of classic lines. *Le Tapis* is made of continuous filament nylon, and is available in seven colors and three sizes. This one could be in a blue-green-purple room.

Delightfully abstract, this Danish-import rya rug called *Stil* reminds us strongly of paintings by the Dutch painter Mondrian. Good as an over-the-carpet accent in front of a sofa or hearth in its 4-½ × 6-½-foot size, it is available in five sizes.

Shimmering color in *Crystal Palace,* below, forms massive abstract flowers and leaves in an art nouveau style. It's made of Acrilan acrylic and modacrylic. In its 6-foot circle size, it could serve as the major room accent in many settings.

Area rugs are today's magic carpets.
They help shape space, divide activities, add decorating dash. Best of all, they can be moved to another room or to another home, and so are versatile as well as beautiful.

Your choice of colors and patterns could not be greater. In addition to the "now" designs of contemporary America, modern rug makers are turning to other times and places for inspiration. Many of the jewel-like colors and intricate patterns resemble timeless Persians or Aubussons searched out in old rug or antique shops.

Motifs are derived from the exotic East, from Scandinavia, Renaissance Italy, Spain, 18th-century England and France. They range in size from 3×5 feet to rugs large enough to be called "room size." Take your pick!

Smashing area rug for the budget-conscious can be made in house with carpet samples and glue. For backing, use canvas in the size you want, leaving a 4-inch heading for hemming. Arrange samples for color effects and for contrast of textures.

Bold medallion design, spicy Latin colors, and heavy knotted fringe make *Matineau,* the Spanish-inspired, all-wool Wilton pictured above, a perfect counterpoint for many fashionable furniture styles of today, especially the Mediterranean group.

An area rug can do lots for a room, but it can work against it, too. The picture at top left reveals an all-too-common mistake. The rug is too skimpy. Chairs spill over its edge. And it does not contain the furniture in the grouping. This doesn't mean you can never use a square rug with a round table. "Never" is a word you rarely hear in decorating. "Depends" is one that you will hear, again and again.

A square rug could be used here. It depends on the size of the rug. If it were large enough to cover almost the whole surface of the floor, then it would become part of the structural harmony and not depend on the table's shape.

The present arrangement leads to two disasters: uncomfortable guests and scratches on the floor.

An area rug's primary function is to define space. The round rug at bottom left is right in size and shape. It is large enough to keep all the chairs within its bounds even when they're pushed back. The round shape echoes that of the dining table and creates a pleasant island.

The color of the rug is right, too. It repeats the colors found on the chair seats. It has been chosen from the warm family, which is harmonious with the gold walls and the wood tones of the furniture. It also supplies accent and contrast.

The floor is in good condition. The color of the rug and its size allow the natural beauty of the wood-grained pattern to be shown off to advantage.

The delightful room at the right is a classic example of area ▶ rugs used to perfection. Here the two area rugs work together to provide unification, dramatization, and repetition for the room and its furnishings.

The large rectangular area rug binds the entire room into one working element, while the small Oriental rug further emphasizes and unifies the conversation grouping and, in addition, provides a beautiful conversation piece within itself.

Area rug do's

Do use for color, plain, or patterned, or to introduce pattern into a dull room—let them soften severe lines—choose to supply texture and match other furnishings—frame those that look like textured paintings—buy for quality in heavily traveled areas—switch them from room to room for variety—try real or imitation fur rugs for a touch of luxury.

Area rug don'ts

Don't bring unrelated colors into one room—pick bold patterns for patterned floors or solid colors for unpatterned rooms—have velvety textures on shaggy wall-to-wall carpet—use two colors in a small room or on marred floors—place a pad under a thick rug—buy cheaper rugs for heavily traveled areas—place rugs kitty-corner to room lines.

Furniture

Less often considered as room accents than pictures, sculpture, ceramic pieces, and the like are the small and highly decorative items of furniture such as cube tables, footstools, floor cushions, that depart enough in style from other room furnishings to stand out.

Kind to budgets indeed are the furniture accent pieces you can make yourself—such as the cube tables below or the floor cushions opposite. Pieces of this kind can, however, be purchased—in many colors, varieties, and in contemporary styles.

Another excellent source for such pieces is the re-sale shop that deals in real and near-antiques. Look for Victorian tables or stools, sectional screens, miniscule chests.

Lighthearted cube coffee tables add a springtime lightness to a contemporary room setting. To get the marbleized effect with paint, start with flat black enamel on wood as an under-coat. When this is dry, paint on white glazing liquid or flat white (or cream) enamel thinned half and half with turpentine. Next crumple a piece of plastic drip cloth, shake it out, and lay it on the glaze. Leave some wrinkles in the cloth. Pick it up carefully so as not to blur the resulting pattern. When this coat has dried, you will be ready—if you wish—to decorate with freehand designs, with stencils, or with paste-on pieces cut from colored paper. When your decorations are completely dry, spray the entire piece with a clear finish.

How to use floor cushions

Floor cushions have become stylish in recent years, due in part to our greater interest in the arts and cultures of various Oriental countries, where they have long been a major item of home furnishing.

As accessories, they are available ready-made in a gorgeous array of coverings—silk, damask, as well as more durable fabrics—and in a rainbow assortment to match or contrast with your overall color scheme.

A small budget may lead you to consider making your own floor cushions. You can purchase foam rubber in many shapes and qualities, or get pillows filled with other man-made or natural stuffing; cover them in fabric to match an upholstered piece, draperies, slip covers, or to contrast in color and texture.

Use them as footstools, or as extra seating; stack in pairs and trios as accents.

A room furnished in eclectic style—borrowing designs from a wide assortment of traditions—and stacks of floor cushions help carry out an overall exotic flavor of decor.

Covered in rosy-hued fabric, they are well related to the deeper hue used as trim and shelving color for the interesting piece at left; and they are also attuned to shades included in the afghan laid across a stool that turns an ordinary lounge chair into a chaise longue when desired.

Tassel trimmings such as those used on some of the pillows can be made with embroidery floss, or purchased ready-made in stores that sell upholstery and fancywork supplies.

The extra seating they provide makes floor cushions both utilitarian and decorative. If you've ever been to Japan, eaten in an authentic Japanese restaurant or peered at the furnishings included in movies about Japan, you're already familiar with the versatility of the floor cushion.

Depending on the fabric with which they are covered, they can accent an Oriental decor, look ultra modern, put a colorful splash of color into a neutral scheme, repeat pattern of draperies, slip covers or upholstery in a room of almost any style. Versatile as your imagination lets them be, floor cushions are well worth your consideration as a useful and beautiful room accessory.

On page 99 you saw an example of the decorative use of floor cushions of the kind used in Oriental homes; on page 101 you'll find a modification of the style that may be more comfortable to Westerners.

Make your floor cushions if you'd like them to match a fabric employed elsewhere in the room. You can purchase a basic pillow covered in muslin, to be covered in any material you choose. Or you can purchase the necessary amount of filling (shredded foam is inexpensive, practical) to stuff a case of a size and shape you like; then re-cover in fabric to harmonize with your color scheme.

Classic Japanese floor cushions, from 24 to 30 inches square, are called zabutons. They are covered on each side with four squares of fabric cut on bias and sewn together, with a decorative button at center, and tassels at each of the four corners.

Handstitch one side of your floor cushion covers so you can remove the pillow easily when the cover needs to be cleaned or laundered—as it probably will quite frequently.

If you're an expert needlewoman, a floor cushion covering offers a beautifully practical chance to display stitchery talents.

How to select and use pillows

Pillows used as accents are among the most effective of small accessories. They will be useful to those seated on deep sofas, and will

For hints on the right and wrong way to use grouped pillows as decorative accessories, see the two pictures below. On the right, off-white pillows of gleaming silk inject good textural contrast with sofa upholstery fabric. They do not compete with its interesting pattern but repeat the color of the ceramic lamp base positioned on the end table at the right of the sofa.

Patterned pillows look out of place on a couch that has a design of its own; striped and solid-color covers on the other pillows are not as bad as boldly patterned ones, but still do less decoratively than the paler tone covering of pillows at left. Positioning is poor, and there is no variety of size and shape, as in group at left, to increase the accessory appeal.

also serve as ornaments if chosen with their decorative role carefully in mind.

You may, of course, buy pillows already covered—in a wide range of sizes, shapes and fabrics. The cost will be dependent upon the quality both of the covering and of material used to fill the pillow. Pillows filled with kapok will cost less than those filled with foam rubber or with high-quality down but will not be as resilient.

Both shape and coverings—color, texture, scale—should be taken into account in your selections. For an elegantly covered *chaise longue* or a love seat, you will obviously want pillows of small size. For a big leather sofa in a den or casually furnished family room, choose different pillows—larger and covered in sturdy material. On sofas upholstered in figured fabrics, use pillows of solid colors.

How to use accessories as finishing touches

Accessories are important features of all well-planned decorating schemes. If you think of them only as little finishing touches, you are not getting the best from them. They are important objects in a room. Therefore, it is important that you choose and arrange them with care, for they will then do the job they're intended to do—add life to any setting. But if you let them "just happen," a distracting clutter will be the result.

Accessories poorly proportioned to the space allotted to them cannot enhance a room. They will be as out of place as is a violin playing an oboe solo in a concerto.

You can rob a good accessory of its importance by placing it in the wrong setting. If you have a number of small accessories that need grouping to be most effective, consider placing them in showcases within a wall-hung unit proportionate to their size. They frequently show to best advantage when displayed in this way.

Subtle indebtedness to Oriental themes can be observed in many of the furnishings of this room: grass cloth on walls, chest and low table that are Japanese in inspiration, and the castor-equipped floor cushion covered in a fabric that is also clearly influenced by Oriental designs in its colorings and pattern. (It will be worth the extra investment to have fabric covering of a piece like this treated to resist soil and stains.)

Not only is a floor cushion of this kind a decided decorative asset, it is also extremely practical in a home or apartment where space is limited but extra guest seating is sometimes required. Notice that the mounted cushion has been so designed that it will roll out of the way and underneath the low bench-chest which occupies one wall.

Depending upon the size of the bench, you could store two to six pieces of this kind in an out-of-the-way position.

Flowers and Plants

Ornaments for rooms you live in—this is one important function of growing plants or arrangements of cut flowers. Perhaps you're in search of bold form; or maybe it's color that you are after. Whatever you want done decoratively, there are plants or flowers to do it for you.

Foliage plants, because they are—or can be—so long lasting, should receive primary consideration as a means of bringing needed accents to a decorating scheme. Think first of the place in the room that most needs the accent of a green and growing plant. Is it in full sun, good light, a dim corner? This will largely determine your choice, unless you are willing to move the plant daily to the right location its variety requires, then back to the spot where you want its decorative value for evening hours.

How to decide what size plant to use

Do you need a tubbed beauty that's 4, 5 or more feet tall? Or do you want a plant to set on a table or chest, not over a foot tall? Scale will be important to the effectiveness, so look at the setting you have in mind with this factor in view. A small plant will be lost in a location that calls for something impressive; and a tall or bushy one will have an unpleasantly crowded look unless it is given an appropriate placement.

Texture, too, deserves thought. If much of the setting (fabrics, furniture finishes, or flooring) has sheen, a lacy or furry look in the foliage plant will present good contrast. Or, if furnishings are napped, mat finish, the glossier the foliage the better its effect will be.

If you lack experience as an indoor gardener, plan a visit to a large greenhouse that grows a wide variety of foliage plants. See what kinds are available to choose from.

Talk to the grower about light, water and humidity requirements. If you're told a plant must have strong light, don't buy it for a location in your home that you know is dimly lit even in daytime hours. Conversely, pass up those that require low light if the spot in your home that needs decorating is next to an expanse of windows facing south. Your plant will soon be sunburned.

The right plant in the right setting, with proper care, will live a long, healthy life.

A graceful Boston fern, accompanied by a glossy-leaved begonia, plus an arrangement of cut flowers nearby add greatly to the inviting character of this living room. Grouping plants is a device worth remembering, for you can often get the "big" effect you want with several medium-sized plants placed next to each other. Each one alone would be interesting but would do little decoratively. Together, they're impressive.

Ferns and begonias both like strong light but not full, hot sun. Both require fairly high humidity in surrounding atmosphere. If you live in a cold climate and your home is warmed for many months with central heat, you will almost certainly have to supply extra moisture to keep plants growing healthily. Do this by setting plants onto pebbles covering bottom of a metal, watertight tray; add water to level of pebble layer.

How to select the proper container

Display with artistry the plants that will play a long-time decorating role in a proper setting. It may take a little time and ingenuity on your part to select containers and accessories in harmony with the plants and with your decorating scheme. But you will have added a personal touch to the natural beauty of plants in a way that is creative, unique, satisfying.

Don't think you have to go out and buy everything that's required. Look at familiar household belongings with a fresh eye. A seldom-used tray, fruit bowl or a metal wastebasket may be a handsome accompaniment to plants.

How to choose the right plant

Big-foliage plants in the right setting are living, growing decorations. With interesting forms, they are as effective a room accent as a piece of sculpture. And many of those that are large enough will tolerate relatively low light.

Among favorites in this group are rubber plants, schefflera, monstera and philodendron grown on a moss stick, diffenbachia and an underrated old standby, sansevieria (rudely nicknamed mother-in-law's tongue).

When the plant is to be placed where its container is seen, remember that the kind of cache-pot will make a big difference in its effectiveness. Containers are to plants what mats and frames are to pictures.

Without the lush, shining green beauty of a tall schefflera plant, this room would be lacking a needed note of natural, casual, but graceful form. Fabric and flooring are interestingly patterned in very regular designs that are all the most appealing because of the contrast with the free form of a big plant. Its shining texture, too, offers good contrast to the mat finish of wall surfaces that supply background.

This plant will live over months and years in a medium-light setting. The greatest danger is overwatering, especially for plants in big pots. Water thoroughly, not too frequently.

Flower and fruit arrangements to greet family and guests when they enter your home speak eloquently of beauty and hospitality. The familiar phrase—"say it with flowers"—is meaningful because flowers *do* say the special things for which it's often difficult or impossible to find the right words.

Everyone likes flowers or a bowl of well-arranged fruit on the table. They please the eye, help whet the appetite, say that this meal—with or without any invited guests—is a special event. For the sharing of food should be a gracious occasion, not a concession to the human need to eat.

Think of color first when you're selecting flowers for the table. They may match, harmonize or contrast with colors of china, linens, glassware and still create a delightful effect. But let it be clear that flower colors are part of a considered color scheme, not a happenstance matter.

Don't feel that everything on your table must "match"; but it must "belong." Shape and size are also significant. Symmetrical centerpieces are the usual choice if those who will dine are to be seated at the sides and ends of the table. Flowers to be arranged this way should be equally attractive from all angles, and the centerpiece should be kept low enough so that each person at the table can see all others without an uncomfortable craning of necks.

Finally think scale: Let the bouquet be in proportion to the table it decorates.

A pleasant variation on the usual centerpiece is this undulating line of flowers and greenery that stretches the full length of the dining table. The mechanics of such arrangements are a little more complicated than for one in a single container—bowls or low vase—where it is a simple matter to supply water to keep flowers fresh. But the trick is not too complex.

One way is to make a shallow container of the desired length and shape with the use of heavy-duty aluminum foil. Remember, though, that all shiny metal must be obscured with foliage or with an overlayer of dull green foil such as florists use to wrap potted plants. Into the homemade foil container, put pieces of water-soaked oasis or other foamlike substance intended to supply cut flowers with a constant amount of moisture. Arrange flowers and foliage by inserting stems in foam.

Another way, and more satisfactory if you would like to use arrangements of this kind fairly often, is to have a tinsmith make you a permanent and watertight long, low container of the proportions you desire. Paint its outside with dull-finish green paint. You can then use needlepoints and water to secure flowers and foliage and keep them supplied with moisture.

In addition to its interesting foam, this arrangement of flowers is pleasing because of its harmony with the total color scheme. Both place mats and upholstered cushions on the chairs are in shades of orange and gold with which the bronzy single chrysanthemums are well coordinated.

There's really no need ever to do without some sort of table ▶ decoration when it's so simple to compose one with the fruits so readily available in the grocery stores. And they cost not a penny—as decorations—since they'll be consumed after they have served their purpose as ornaments.

Bowls of lemons only, red apples, oranges—what you will—are as attractive as mixtures. And you needn't stop with fruit. Many vegetables make equally attractive table decorations. Try red, ripe tomatoes with parsley for foliage, or squashes of several shapes and colors, or purple and white onions.

Needless to say, such arrangements shouldn't be confined to a kitchen or dining room. Many can move to the living room or family room and do much to accent your color scheme.

Light fixtures and lighting effects

Skilled use of light makes for dramatic decorating. Whether in the form of lamps, light fixtures, or indirect lighting, new ways with illumination needn't cost a fortune. Don't make the mistake of assuming that unusual lighting effects must carry a high price tag. Tiffany-style ceiling fixtures similar to the one below can sometimes be found cheaply when older houses are demolished for freeways.

And good reproductions are available at modest prices.

Concealed lighting effects often take a larger amount of imagination than of money. Variations on the theme are exciting: behind a valance where light will be cast on a wall of draperies; under strategically located cornices that extend out from the wall to hide tubes or bulbs (this trick can be used to visually raise a low ceiling); soffit lighting in kitchens and baths; especially, where illumination kind to the eye but adequate in brightness is desired, in a wall or ceiling, luminous panels light a sizable area of a room. The list of ways to put concealed lighting to work as an aid to decorating schemes could go on and on. Study our examples for a fresh approach.

Elegantly appointed, eclectic in feeling, this highly individual living room, right, owes more than a little of its character to the unusual lighting effects that are an integral part of its decorating scheme. A black column behind the sofa has a square of frosted glass for a top, with light thrown upward and onto an urn containing an interesting foliage plant. It might serve equally well to spotlight a piece of sculpture.

Concealed lighting at floor level gains intensity and importance when it is reflected onto a mirrored folding screen like that which separates these living and dining areas.

The style of lighting that will be most effective in your home is the one that is best related to the style of other furnishings. If yours is a home furnished in classic styles, you won't want lighting effects that are anachronistic in an obvious way. You needn't use only candles for an Eighteenth Century English-style living room, but you don't want fixtures or techniques that have a "mod" look, either.

As you study the illustrations of furnishings in this volume and those to follow, pay special attention to lighting effects that please you. Borrow from those that are congenial to the style of furnishings you have chosen for your home.

Don't be limited by the expected when it comes to using light ▶ and lighting fixtures as important accessories or even as keys to a decorating scheme. There's no creative satisfaction in turning out carbon copies. Unique accessories can quickly transform an ordinary bathroom into an extraordinary one.

Case in point: bath at left, which surprises with a Tiffany-like ceiling fixture and old Godey prints. Related paper border extends around ceiling and, without scallops, is repeated as a dado. To call attention quickly to the most decorative accessory of all—the ceiling light—it has been surrounded by a wallpaper circle of yellow primroses that speak of yesterday.

Look for other unusual light fixtures and lamps as you use this and succeeding volumes. Take note of the way they're employed as important room accessories, not mere utilitarian necessities to shed artificial light when the sun goes down.

Choice pieces of crystal, ceramics, small sculptures are suddenly endowed with greatly increased importance when they're set on shelves that light them from above or below with concealed fixtures hidden inside of shelves or molding. It's an old trick to jewelers, who know how to make their wares irresistible; borrow it to focus attention on your small treasures.

The lighting panel below is great for backlighting accessories. Unit supplying illumination is portable. It plugs into a wall outlet and isn't a permanent installation; thus you can move it to another room or to another home. With a unit like this, you can turn accessories into significant ornaments.

Select the right light for the right place

The right lights in the right places will do for a room what theme music does for a picture—add the punctuation and establish the mood you want.

Light is, or can be if properly used, both an accessory in itself and a means of turning attention dramatically onto a decorative feature deserving important notice.

Lighting comes in many forms: lamps for the end tables, floor lamps, recessed light fixtures, hanging lights, chandeliers, and in luminous wall or ceiling panels, if you're looking for very new effects. All these sources of light can be increased or lessened in intensity when equipped with a rheostat switch.

Don't settle for merely adequate lighting when, with today's fixtures, you can employ lighting as an ornament and an accessory to coordinate with your decorating scheme.

How to balance lighting

Balanced lighting consists of a mixture of the three main types: background, which will wash a room with soft, general illumination; local, which casts light directly onto an area (a work surface, for example), and accent, which spotlights an important accessory or furniture grouping.

Don't settle for overhead fixtures. Without fail you'll find you need more light in more places. The obvious answer is to supplement general lighting with portables.

In the bedroom, the light you need for reading in bed can come from wall-mounted fixtures that will shine onto your book. In kitchens, dining rooms, and elsewhere, a light fixture mounted on a ceiling track is felxible, practical, easy to install.

An ingenious use of light aids in dividing space. The home or ▶ apartment that has no entrance hall, but needs one, might solve its problem this way: with drop blinds that conceal ceiling-high lamps atop spring poles. Light focused straight down gives the screen an effect close to that of a solid wall, but won't shine into the eyes of persons seated anywhere.

ADDITIONS

How To Expand Your House
To Meet Your Growing Needs

Time brings changes. Your family's way of living alters as the years go by. New materials, techniques, and designs come along and make you yearn for modernization. Additions to your family create a need for additions to your house. And as your youngsters grow, so do their interests and possessions. More leisure time and new interests call for modifications in the space that surrounds you.

However, with each passing year, real estate costs also change—climbing higher and higher due to the increasing population and the demand for more land for public use. The supply of land available for residential purposes declines in "near in" areas, and the distances to and from newly developed areas become greater every year.

As a result, more and more homeowners—just like yourself—who need larger homes, or homes better adapted to their living requirements, are finding it easier on their pocketbooks to remodel or add on to their existing homes. Aside from the high costs of land for new construction, many families choose to remodel because of their desire to remain in a familiar, well-liked neighborhood, or of their home's proximity to schools, church, and shopping.

Whatever your reason for adding on that new addition, remember that planning a major renovation is just as involved as planning a new home. So before you decide to add on that addition, take time to be analytical about your present house and your family needs. Sit down and figure out costs and various ways of financing the addition. If possible, get professional help with your design and specific plans. It's a good way to insure your investment.

Take a good look at your home. You will notice that it contains many distinct areas—areas for eating, cooking, sleeping, bathing, relaxing, and entertaining. These different areas should complement one another in order to provide whole-house livability.

Now ask yourself: "Is the kitchen unhandy? The bathroom outdated? Laundry area cramped? Another bedroom needed? More storage space needed everywhere?"

Whatever you decide on, be it a new family room, expanding the kitchen, building a new patio, or any other addition you have in mind—it can only result in one thing: Better living.

Decide on family needs first

Generally, the primary purpose of an addition is to satisfy your family's requirements. The addition should be more than just tacked-on space, it should serve a purpose. It should give your house a new dimension by taking the pressure off crowded areas.

Make a detailed study of your existing house. Take a tour, room by room, with pencil and paper in hand and jot down what you (and the rest of the family) would like to add and where you would like to add it. Look, also, to the future. Make sure your present plans incorporate future needs.

This family room addition is just for grownups. The children have taken over the old living room and a "fun" room downstairs. Comfortable sofas and a generous fireplace with a built-in woodbox supplement the relaxed atmosphere. It supplies room for informal entertaining and quiet evenings.

Books are always close, and shelf-organized. The balcony is at chandelier height. It's wide enough for convenient browsing among the volumes, can even hold a desk if you need to do some research. Cupboards in the middle of the shelves supply storage for games, magazines or records.

Spotlights in the ceiling provide lively lighting to the balcony. The high ceiling helps make the room seem bigger than it really is. The view from the entry is impressive. Space-making white walls contrast with the deep warm colors.

Adding a room is often much the same as moving into a different, and better, home. The new space, especially if it's a family room or other living area, can alter your living habits to such an extent that you'll soon wonder how you lived without it.

Planning for an addition is easier if you collect clippings that picture and describe the ideas you want to include—the kind of paneling, wall colors, fabrics, fireplace detail, floor style, and so on. Once you decide what you want, the clippings can help you visualize what the end result will look like. Also, you'll be reassured during the actual building of the addition and avoid costly last-minute changes caused by indecision.

Keep the exterior simple

When you're planning your addition, think about possible changes you can make to your home's exterior. Oftentimes, an alteration or even several alterations can fit right in with other work. However, just a word of caution—too often, exterior alterations wind up being only changes, not improvements. Your best bet is to avoid a complicated addition. Strive for a simplification of the exterior that helps it attain a modern look.

A good point to remember is that, as a rule of thumb, an addition should slip onto your present exterior as a glove slips on a hand. It should look as though it belongs—as though it came with the house.

Sometimes, an existing structure can form the basis of a new living space. As shown below, an attached garage can be converted into an extra room with only a minimum of change and expense. Windows or sliding glass doors can go where the garage doors are. And there is no need to worry about matching roof lines. Some readjustment of landscaping is probably called for in order to tie in the garage with the rest of the front. In addition to the new windows, insulation is necessary to make the room snug. And don't overlook heating and cooling equipment. For example, your furnace might not be adequate and installation of electric heat or separate room heaters may be necessary.

This house (above) had a front porch that was an eyesore. Not only was it uncomfortable and seldom used, but it made the house look old beyond its years. Its façade was lifted by the application of siding and wallboard. The new enclosed porch and entry gave added living space and made the whole house look like new. Since this side of the house faced the street, windows were set high enough to give privacy and still admit sunlight. The front entrance now serves as an entry hall adjacent to the living room. And by enclosing the porch, major dividends were paid both in appearance and in convenience.

A brand-new room (below) was added to the side of this traditional home. The one-story dining room modifies the look of the peaked, box-like structure, helping to make it seem lower. The addition repeats the same lines as the house—but at a lower level. And as the roof line is kept, so is the trim duplicated. The small-paned windows are like those used in the original house—except these wood divisions can be removed when the windows need washing. The same style shutters carry over to surround the big window in the new room. New plantings are placed around the addition.

How to get started

will be worth every dollar in the better working and more pleasing result you'll get in your addition.

How to plan an addition

No addition should be planned until the entire house has been studied. A good addition should revitalize all areas of your present house and make living more enjoyable.

As mentioned earlier, make an inspection trip through your house and list your comments on a sheet of paper. In the bedroom area, make notes about the adequacy of closets, room for children to study, play area, amount of floor space, furniture needs, windows, lighting fixtures, everything and anything that comes to mind. Check the bath while you're in the bedroom area.

The same kind of notes should be made for family living space, dining area, entry, and any special-purpose rooms. Don't forget storage space; it's one of the best items to include in an addition. From all these notes, you'll be able to define what your house needs to bring it up to your expectations.

"Secondary" shortcomings can usually be solved with a smart addition. For instance, you can often plan a whole wall of closets when you change interior walls—at very little cost and loss of floor space. A new front entry that's more dramatic and serviceable can be a by-product of your rearrangement of interior space. Also, a different placement of interior doorways could eliminate existing traffic jams and inconvenience.

Now is your chance to change the exterior appearance of your house. Styling changes come easily when you're building on. Your final plans shouldn't be made without considering this point. Also, the experience and help of an architect assures you of best results. Many remodeling contractors offer free planning help and employ trained architects. At any rate, an architect's fee isn't high—and it

How to choose a contractor

When your planning's done and you are certain that the addition will make your house right for you, it's time to start shopping for a contractor. Don't rush this step because both your money and your comfort are at stake. You can get contractors' names from friends who have remodeled, from trade associations, from bank references, and from the telephone directory. Look at their completed work before making any decision. Get bids from at least two, but don't take the lowest one without making sure you will be satisfied with the kind of work you'll get.

Two essentials are: (1) a firm estimate of the time required; and (2) complete agreement and understanding with the builder on all details. Talk about everything—from the price of light fixtures and new appliances to the brand and type of windows and the quality of hardware you want him to use. Detailed discussions like this will forestall misunderstandings that can easily develop later.

And before signing the contract, make sure it spells out in writing a detailed cost estimate, the total price, the terms of payment, any provision for changes during construction (the more you make, the more your job costs), approximate completion date, and the responsibilities and liens of the subcontractors. It's also wise to arrive at some understanding about callbacks once the job is finished. A responsible contractor stands in back of his work for at least a year following the completion of the job. You should be fair, too; a contractor should not have to correct faults beyond his control.

When you're completely satisfied—with both the price and the quality of work your contractor offers—sign the agreement.

How to finance your addition

Ideas for rewarding home improvement additions are too often scuttled because the costs, when tallied, would cripple the family budget. Such an obstacle as securing a loan isn't as limiting amd penalizing as it seems. There's an easy way to turn your remodeling hopes and needs into substance and reality: Monthly payment financing.

Here are seven common home improvement financing programs. The availability and terms of any of these plans vary according to geographic location. Even Federal Housing Administration practices differ according to regional office. Actually, the FHA does not lend money to homeowners. Loans are made by lending institutions; the FHA merely insures the loan.

(1) *FHA Property Improvement Loan* (Title I). Under this plan you may borrow up to $5,000 and take up to 7 years, 32 days to pay. To qualify, your improvements must be "built-in" or of such a kind that they become a permanent part of the property. Owners of multiple-unit dwellings may borrow up to $2,500 per dwelling unit, with up to 7 years to pay back the loan.

(2) *FHA Section 203 (k) Loan* (Title II). This program was devised for improving older homes. If your home is over 10 years old, you can finance improvements costing up to $10,-000 and take up to 20 years to pay. The loan to cover the remodeling is secured by a second mortgage on the property.

(3) *Conventional Bank Installment Loan.* This kind of loan is usually more flexible than FHA loans as to purpose, the amount loaned, and the terms of repayment; you may include improvements such as the addition of appliances that are not built in. In addition to commercial and savings banks, many savings and loan associations now offer this type of installment loan.

(4) *Open-end Mortgage Loan.* If you have an open-end mortgage on your present home, you may be able to finance your improvements by borrowing more money on the same mortgage—though not always at the same interest rate of your original loan.

(5) *Mortgage Refinancing.* You may be able to retire your present mortgage, and get another in a larger amount to include the cost of your improvements. The desirability of this alternative depends upon the terms; compare the interest rate and the terms of a new mortgage against those of your present one. In the case of an extensive improvement, refinancing may be the only answer. Refinancing may be accomplished under either conventional or FHA auspices. Under FHA 203 (b), mortgage financing is available up to $30,000, with up to 30 years to pay back the money borrowed.

(6) *New Mortgage.* If you have no mortgage indebtedness, you may obtain a mortgage on the property to make improvements. And if you are a prospective owner of an older home that needs extensive modernization, you can save money by combining the cost of the home and the cost of the modernization into the mortgage.

(7) *Dealer Financing.* Use your credit with your building material dealer. He may be a member of a charge plan or have his own credit program. If you are dealing with a remodeling contractor, he might be able to arrange financing for both the materials needed and the labor involved in the improvement.

Planning

Once you've decided on the type of addition you want, the contractor, and how you are going to finance the remodeling—there are still two very important problems to consider while you are still in the planning stages. These are your heating and wiring systems. A new addition might be just too much for your old furnace to handle effectively, and the new electrical appliances and lighting could be a dangerous overload on your wiring system. So this is the point for you to check these problems and to do something about them.

Think about adding climate control

Comfort control in older homes is a far cry from the sophisticated systems available today. Now there's more to it than an operating furnace in winter, and open windows in summer. And when building that new addition, you can make your vintage heating system easier to live with, and add most of the elements of modern climate control. Or, if necessary, install a completely new heating system and/or a supplementary heating unit.

Have your heating contractor give your present heating system a complete inspection, cleaning, and adjustment. If yours is a forced-air system, you can greatly improve the comfort level in your home and cut your heating bills—even with a new addition—by having everything balanced for even heating of all rooms, and by adjusting the blower for continuous operation.

Naturally, you need a new furnace if a major breakdown dictates complete replacement, but there are other factors that might make a new furnace worthwhile, too. For instance, if you have an old coal furnace converted to gas or oil, it probably takes up basement space that you could put to better use. And an old furnace that requires constant repair is a prime candidate for replacement, particularly if the new installation can include central air conditioning.

How to shop for a new system

Don't simply buy a furnace; seize the opportunity, when adding on a new addition, to upgrade the climate all over your house. Start shopping before your building plans are too far along to alter or before your present furnace has breathed its last. Visit the showrooms of several heating contractors, compare the brands they handle, and make an evaluation of their service facilities. Pick up manufacturers' brochures and take them home. Study them carefully; take detailed notes.

Then narrow the field down to two or three contractors; invite each of them to give an estimate. First, the contractor's representative may make a quick tour of the major rooms, then depart for the basement. Down there, he scans the specifications plate on your present furnace, if you're replacing one.

His time is valuable, and he has learned from experience that many homeowners aren't interested in hearing about BTUs and mathematical formulas. They just want to know costs. But you should explain that you are interested—and that quality is just as important as money. Emphasize that you want an estimate for a top-notch system. But be sure to have the contractor itemize the estimate so you can go over it later, and you can decide what to do without or to postpone until later. That way you can tailor the job to your budget.

With these instructions, a good estimator will start working harder. After determining the size of your present house in square feet plus the addition you plan to build, he'll note ceiling heights, number of windows, and the location of supply registers and air returns.

Tell him how your present furnace has

performed. Are certain rooms chilly or too warm? Do people get shocked by static electricity every time they touch a doorknob? How do your fuel bills compare with your neighbors'? With these answers and some data on your house, the estimator can give you a thorough analysis.

"If you really want to go first-class," he begins cautiously, "I'd recommend what we call a total comfort system. That includes a furnace, central air conditioner, power humidifier, and an electronic air cleaner."

Don't be alarmed at the list of equipment he's reciting. The total price for it could come to well over $1,000, but you only need to buy the basics at first. And notice that now he's speaking in terms of a "system," not just a furnace. You should think that way, too.

"Your furnace," the estimator continues, "should be rated at 125,000 BTUs. If winters were very cold here, or this house had high ceilings or poor insulation, that BTU requirement would be a lot higher. Your house measures about 2,000 square feet, and you need about 50 BTUs per square foot." He's right on all points, though his arithmetic may seem peculiar. That's because furnaces are identified by their input ratings, which tell how much heat they produce internally. But the figure that counts most is the output rating—how much heat a furnace actually delivers.

A well-designed gas or oil furnace normally works at about 80 percent efficiency—so a unit rated at 125,000 BTUs delivers about 100,000 BTUs of usable heat. To be sure the bids you're getting are truly competitive, specify that all estimates be based on output ratings.

"Now let me tell you about the cooling part of a total comfort system," the estimator says. "A 40,000 BTU unit ought to do a good job for you. But I'm afraid we'll have to do some extra work on your supply ducts. They just aren't large enough to carry cold air effi-

ciently." In most areas, a system needs bigger carrying capacity for cool air than for warm.

Ductwork is sometimes expensive, but you can stretch out the cost of a complete system by having the sheet metal work done when the new furnace is installed, then waiting a summer or two before buying the cooling unit itself.

Cold air holds less moisture than warm air, so if winters in your area are cold enough for heating, you need a humidifier of some sort. Evaporative humidifiers can put up to three or four gallons of water a day into the air—enough for mild cold spells or small houses. But if it gets colder, or your house is bigger, you may need as much as 16 gallons of water a day in the air—and that's a job for a power humidifier.

Although the power humidifier will help some, there are two other simple modifications that will help even more. The first is to add a fresh air intake. All you need is a short duct from the return air plenum to the outside, with a damper for controlling the flow of fresh air into the system. The second modification is to set up a furnace blower for continuous air circulation. The blower operates at a slower speed than the one in your present furnace, but it runs all the time, moving air whether the heat is on or not.

And, finally, by putting an electronic air cleaner into the return plenum of your furnace, you can remove up to 95 percent of the airborne dust in your home.

While the estimator totals up all the items, make sure he's including an installation guarantee, a yearly maintenance contract, and free call-back service for balancing and adjustment just after the work has been done.

Keep in mind that a central air conditioner, electronic filter, and even a power humidifier are generally add-on units you can have installed later. So if you don't buy all the equipment at once, hold onto that estimate.

What you should know about wiring

If you're building a new addition, chances are great that it will be necessary to rewire your home. Rewiring is one of those home improvements you can't see, but it pays off in safety and convenience. Insufficient and inefficient wiring plagues you with blown fuses, slow-heating appliances, flickering television every time an appliance goes on, and a welter of unsightly and dangerous extension cords over. Rewiring your home may be costly, but the savings in improved efficiency are many.

If that new addition is a workshop, you'll need a branch circuit, and a second circuit if you use heavier power tools. A branch circuit breaker, while not absolutely necessary, can give you easy and reachable control over equipment. It helps protect the main service panel from circuit overloads; and you can break the current before you leave the shop as an added safety measure. Often you'll lose much of the efficiency that power tools provide if you can't use them where you need them. So when wiring, make sure you place convenient outlets all around the perimeter of your workshop.

How to check your electrical system

Check your wiring first where the electrical power comes into your house—through a service panel known as an entrance box (see diagram). This box contains your fuses or circuit breakers, and the main power shut-off switch. Often the main switch will be labeled with the total number of amperes entering your house. In home wiring today, 100-amp service—24,000 watts—is minimum, and even then you have little or no margin on which to operate all your family portable appliances.

Check the number and amperage rating of the various electric circuits. This data in older homes may be tucked away in unlikely places, so do a little hunting to find it all. The former owners may have replaced fuses with new ones of a higher amperage, to avoid the inconvenience of constantly blown fuses. This is a very dangerous practice—almost as bad as replacing burned-out fuses with pennies—since a fuse is a safety valve to protect against circuit overload. Most older homes are wired with number 14 wire requiring 15-amp fuses—so be suspicious of any 20- or 30-amp fuses you find, especially if your home has never had any new circuits added.

How to plan rewiring

If your new addition is being attached to an older home, rewiring can mean anything from bringing in new and heavier entrance wires, a new breaker panel, and extensive in-wall repairs and new circuits, down to the simple addition of a circuit or two to beef up your present system. When installing new wiring, however, electrical contractors in many areas are required by law to bring your entire electrical system up to minimum safety standards.

When planning your new wiring, specify a system with the following circuits: (1) general purpose circuits for lighting, with additional outlets to eliminate all those extension cords; (2) small-appliance circuits to the kitchen, laundry, bathrooms, and dining area; (3) separate lighting and power circuits, if you have or are building an extensive workshop, for all your power tools and special lighting needs; (4) additional individual circuits for major appliances—air conditioners, washer, freezer, hot water heater, range, clothes dryer.

Make a diagram of the complete wiring system and mount it on the inside of the fuse box or breaker-panel door. All new circuits should be number 12 wire, for full 20-amp circuits. Major appliances should have the wire size, voltage, and amperage tailored to their needs. With such a diagram you can easily locate and replace a fuse without plunging the house into darkness.

Unless you have some special problems, the cost of rewiring will probably fall within the $300-$500 range. The cost of extending a single 220-volt line for a major appliance will be about $40, with another $15 fee if the line goes to the second floor of the house.

These are characteristics of a well-wired home. It has a three-wire service entrance with a circuit breaker or main switch of at least 100-amperes. A 200-ampere entrance is even better. Branch circuits may be seen coming from the main circuit box. The ones shown here include a general purpose circuit (green) for every 500 square feet of space for lights and convenience outlets. These include appliances such as television sets and electric blankets as well as appliances used only occasionally, like hair dryers and irons. The small appliance circuit (yellow) is intended largely for kitchen items. For maximum efficiency, you need at least two of these circuits. Larger items, such as the furnace, washer and water heater need individual circuits for each appliance.

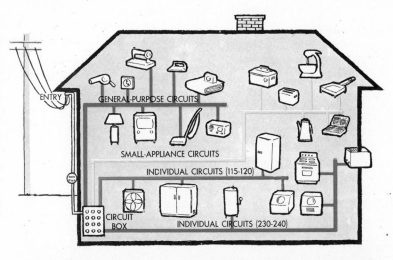

A wiring diagram for the workshop (this one is 10 × 16 feet) might be planned in this manner. Four circuits are controlled from a branch panel. The two lighting circuits (yellow) insure good lighting where you need it. A separate circuit (green) is used to run portable power tools and other equipment. A heavy-duty circuit (blue) takes care of bigger power tools. Small-load power tools are used on the 110/120-volt circuit. Heavier tools need a circuit of 230/240 volts for the best setup. One ½-horsepower motor is all that can be operated efficiently on a 15-amp circuit. The wire to this outlet should be at least number 14 for this kind of a load. If the total wire run to the main-entrance panel is more than 50 feet, use number 12 heavy cord. For large tools, heavier wire with a rubber coating is a must. Take these precautions to avoid trouble.

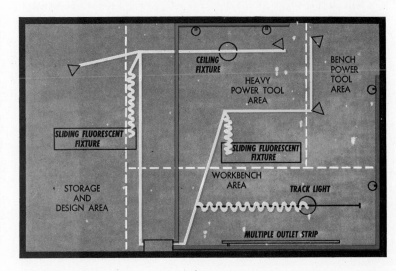

The feeder line to this branch control panel comes in at the top. It is connected to the electric meter and provides power control for the shop circuits only. When you leave the workshop you can turn off the main switch and lock the panel door to make sure no one, especially youngsters, can use the power tools or the lights when you are not there. You don't even have to turn off the lights; the switch does it for you.

To estimate the amperage your circuits should ideally carry, check the amperage listed on the motor nameplate of your tool, then double this amount. The average for most shop-circuit requirements is about 20 amperes. Using too small a wire in a circuit can cause the motor to overheat.

This branch control panel has four active circuits and two spares, six circuits all together. The heavy-duty circuit uses a double breaker, and it is split-wired to carry both 110 and 220 volts. Number 12 heavy, rubber-covered wire is used for runs of more than 25 feet. Heavy wire is a better choice for larger motors even for short runs. For runs longer than 50 feet to the main panel, use number 12 wire to be on the safe side.

If you install new shop outlet boxes, make sure that they are grounded. This type of special outlet receives either a two- or three-prong plug. The grounding prong is connected to a metal conduit whose grounding requirements are specified in local wiring codes. If in doubt, check what the code specifies.

Lighting the workshop is particularly important. You need proper light anywhere you are working. For close-up jobs, you can rig a concentrated light to help you save time and cut eye strain. A goose-neck lamp has the advantage of being movable in many directions so you can get light right where you need it. You can buy a new one or convert an old desk lamp. A small high-intensity lamp would be adequate for smaller jobs, but it is too low for larger work. You might rig a higher stand for one if that is more convenient. The goose-neck lamp or a high-intensity lamp with a stand can be secured by clamping it to the workbench with the kind of a clamp you'd use to hold a glued furniture joint together. Then if you happen to bump it, it won't fall.

A track light above the workbench is mobile and still shines down upon the work you're doing. You can make it as the fluorescent fixture described above, only plan it so the height is just your size. Use a heavy-duty cord for the light. In fact, beware of "piano wire" drop cords for all your equipment. Undersized wires are probably responsible for more burned-out motors than any other factor. Your heavy-duty tools must have a large enough cord. The dealer who sells you the power tools can supply the exact cord required. You also need heavier cord (number 12, rubber-covered) for runs to convenience outlets that are more than 25 feet long. For larger motors and longer runs, heavier wire is essential. Electricity is so important to living and working, you can't afford to take a chance.

You can install stationary fixtures over your permanently installed pieces of equipment. Buy fixtures with reflecting shades that diffuse the light over a wide enough area so no part of the power equipment is in shadow. A silver-tipped bulb also helps spread out the light for general illumination. Don't depend on 25- or even 60-watt bulbs to give you the light you need. Buy bulbs with enough wattage to give adequate light. When you buy switches, wiring and outlets, choose those that display the Underwriters Laboratory seal of approval. Always be sure your hands and the floor are dry before you plug in electrical equipment or touch the light switch. If repairs are needed, pull the plug or shut off the current first.

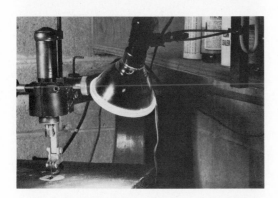

Another inexpensive source of concentrated light for your workshop can be made by using a flood light bulb held firmly in a photography clamp. It provides enough light to overcome the stroboscopic effect of fluorescent lights which can be hard on your eyes and allow you to make mistakes. If a fuse blows, replace it with a new one of the same ampere rating. Putting pennies or foil behind dead fuses is risky business. Another safety feature when dealing with frayed ends of appliance cords is to wrap asbestos or cotton string around the frayed insulation before you re-attach it. Electrical tape prevents a break in the cord covering from giving you a shock. If you run into an electrical problem that you are unable to solve, consult an electrician rather than take a chance on a make-shift solution.

A sliding fluorescent fixture provides fine general illumination for your workshop. You can make a slide for the fixture with two wooden hangers and a length of conduit. Drill holes in the hangers for the conduit. Attach the wooden hangers to the ceiling with brackets, then thread the conduit through the hangers. Attach the hanging cord with rings that slip over the conduit. You can use drapery rings such as those that are made for shower or cafe curtains. Space the rings evenly along the cord so that when you slide them to the side they form half loops. These loops (when pushed to the side) provide a good way to protect the cord from bends that might break it, and also keep it out of your way. Hang the lamp high enough so you won't bump your head on it.

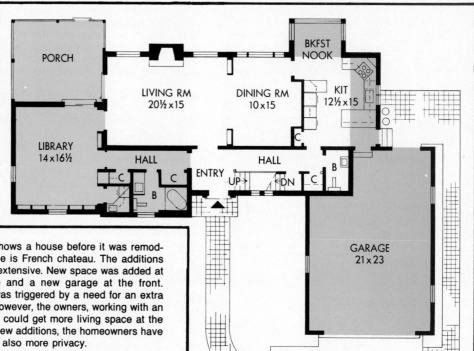

PORCH

LIVING RM
20½ x 15

DINING RM
10 x 15

BKFST
NOOK

KIT
12½ x 15

LIBRARY
14 x 16½

HALL

HALL

ENTRY

UP

DN

C

B

B

C

C

C

GARAGE
21 x 23

This picture, upper left, shows a house before it was remodeled. Its architectural style is French chateau. The additions made to this home were extensive. New space was added at both ends of the house and a new garage at the front. Initially, the remodeling was triggered by a need for an extra bath and a new garage. However, the owners, working with an architect, discovered they could get more living space at the same time. And with the new additions, the homeowners have not only more space, but also more privacy.

In this layout, upper right, the shaded part of the plan marks the outlines of the new rooms added to the original home. The kitchen and breakfast nook were enlarged when the new garage was being constructed. The new bath was placed at the front of the house. An office-library, which could double as a guestroom with convenient bath facilities nearby, was also added. The old porch was on the side of the house; now the new one is concealed from a front view and gives more privacy in the back and also a better view.

Shown below, you can see how the French chateau styling is preserved in the design of the additions. Comparing the 'before' and 'after,' the home now appears more gracious and luxurious. The French styling looks more authentic, and clever landscaping has blended the new sections with the old. The new roof appears a little lighter than the old one, but the wood shingles will weather darker before long. The house is a good example of how additions can result in better living.

Multi-purpose rooms

If the same addition-improvement project were carried out in a hundred homes, it's probable that there would be a hundred different results. Each family would adapt the project according to its likes and manner of living. And this is especially true when it comes to multi-purpose rooms.

In today's busy family living centers, flexibility is especially important. Few modern families can afford, in expense or space, a room that serves only one function. And this is where the multi-purpose room comes in; it's versatile enough to handle many family activities. With simple additions, you can make practically every room in your house multifunctional.

The library shown below is a spacious room, measuring 14 × 16½ feet. Here, looking into the front corner, are two built-in bookcases with cabinet space below for storage. The windows are large and require draperies, since they are on the front and side of the remodeled house. Oak paneling, which takes little maintenance, covers the walls and book-shelves. The paneling on the cabinet doors is cut diagonally for ornamental interest. The uses of this type of addition are almost endless. It provides office space if you need it, or serves as a family room or den. A sofa that can be converted into a bed makes the room ideal as a guest bedroom. And the new bath makes it especially convenient for guests.

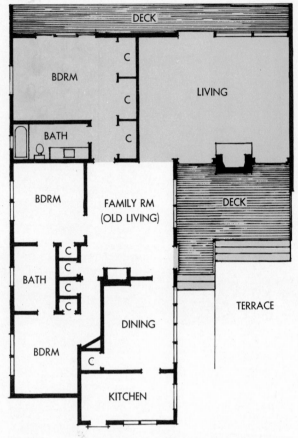

New additions turned this small, traditional style house into a modern home that incorporates outdoor living areas. The original house had 925 square feet of floor space. A new living room and master bedroom suite (shown in the shaded areas of the plan above) almost doubled the living space to 1,620 square feet. Decks were also added to give even more usable space. The original living space remained virtually untouched, and the old living room with a fireplace made a fine multi-purpose living area. The new closets in the bedroom practically doubled the amount of closet space in the entire house. The large bedroom, with an open view, has its own bath. The new living room is equipped for outdoor and indoor entertaining.

How to plan a multi-purpose room

If your family is really cramped for space, and you're planning an addition, think big. Forget the labels—dining room, bedroom, living room, and so on—think of multi-purpose rooms, or if you prefer, living-family centers.

In light of the high investment you already have in your home and in light of the steadily rising costs of new homes, you owe it to yourself and your family to make the best use of all your home's present—and potential—living space. If your family needs more elbow-room, a well-placed addition in the form of a multi-purpose room could be a most rewarding and economic answer.

Let's say, for example, that you need to add on an extra bedroom. Well now, with more leisure time to deal with, and almost constant sources of communication and entertainment, you may occasionally need some apart-ness. And so, the function of the new bedroom could be broadened to that of a personal living room. It should be a room equipped not only for sleeping or homework, but also for pursuing completely personal activities such as reading, hobbies, or just plain daydreaming. And, if you make the new bedroom addition just a few feet longer or a few feet wider than ordinary size, you can plan for a built-in wall of storage and counter space, or a cozy sitting area with a fireplace. And don't hesitate to liven up the decorating—you can sleep just as well in a smartly decorated room; and the waking hours you spend there will be much more enjoyable and relaxing.

But, say you need a specific type of new space and can't add it just where it's needed. The answer: add an addition of a different type, and reassign functions of existing spaces or rooms. For example, let's say you need a family room that should be near the kitchen. But the kitchen is surrounded by your present living room and dining room and you don't have enough lot space outside the kitchen for an addition. Solution: add a new living room at the front of the house and convert your present living room into that multi-purpose family room. That's what so nice about a multi-purpose addition; it can be a brand-new addition or it can be made from existing space with only minor remodeling.

In this picture (above), the view is toward the new rear deck and the picturesque scene that the homeowners wanted to emphasize. When the addition was built, big floor-to-ceiling windows and frames were installed. There is no need for drapes, since there's nothing close to them. The lights of San Francisco's Sausalito harbor at night become a heavenly mural for their room. The tongue-and-groove ceiling follows the roof line to give the room a feeling of spaciousness augmented by the light-reflecting walls. The roof extends beyond the house to shelter the deck and window-wall in all types of weather.

Large glass doors in the front wall of this living room swing open wide to integrate indoor and outdoor living areas. The fireplace is built of traditional used brick, but the simple oak frame produces a contemporary look. The hardwood floors were finished to match those in the original house. The bookshelves and cabinet units on the wall have a built-in look; however, they are really fastened to adjustable shelf brackets. The metal strips were buried in the plasterboard, then covered with tape. They were painted at the same time as the walls and are now almost invisible. An area rug draws the furniture in from the walls.

New uses for old rooms

When you are making your inspection tour, don't fall into a sentimental trap. Do not move swiftly through each room, set in your mind that this room cannot change—it has always been the family room, bedroom, or what have you. Sure, maybe it has but it doesn't necessarily have to be in the future. Be objective and imaginative, too. What now might be a bedroom could become the office or den Dad has always yearned for. And then your new addition could be the bedroom. The idea is to look for new uses for old rooms—before you add on that addition, be it inside or out. Be flexible and your rooms will be, too.

Idea in action

To show you that nothing is sacred when it comes to finding new uses for old rooms, let's take a look at how one couple added to their home.

Needing a family room, the couple noticed that their garage was nestled under two beautiful redwood trees. Not only was it a perfect spot for a new family room but it also was a very inexpensive source, too. So, of course, they decided to convert the garage into a new family room.

The garage was already situated near both the living room and kitchen. They extended the front eight feet, so there was additional space for a library-guest room. They retained the back slope of the garage roof so that the family room exists within the original structure of the garage. The roof peak was raised so that the pitch of the roof over the addition would repeat that of the main roof.

The car? It's not out in the cold. A new carport under the same roof line now shelters it in great style.

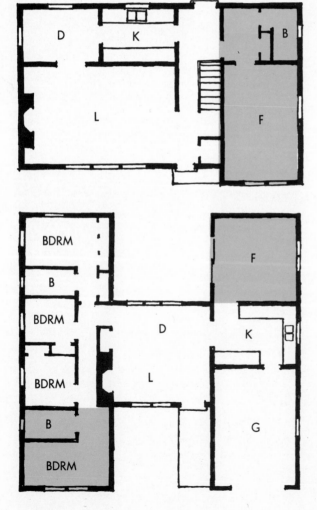

Once you decide on the addition you need, start looking for a connecting link. In the upper left plan, the most natural place to add on the family room is near the kitchen. This is very practical because of the convenience in serving snacks and meals there. Also, you are close enough to supervise the children's play from the kitchen. Another dividend in this type of arrangement is that you have a bathroom near the back door—convenient to both family room and kitchen. And the small entry room next to the bath is ideal for laundry equipment, a place to keep boots and coats, and to dress the young ones.

In the lower left plan, a family room was added right next to the kitchen—again, the kitchen being the connecting link. Later, when the homeowners decided to add on an extra bedroom, they took advantage of the present zoning of the house. Most bedroom additions require the creation of a hallway to provide access to the new room. It's usually wise to choose one of the larger bedrooms (as shown in this plan) so that the loss of space won't make the room too small. As an added bonus, this plan includes a master-bedroom bath.

Handmade Mexican brick and vertical redwood siding combine in the new façade. Strong, solid masses and boldly defined lines make this new face highly individual. Not only is the exterior striking in its simplicity, but it also provides privacy for the interior. On the upper story, redwood louvers partially mask the remaining two bedroom windows. Their full-story height is intended to keep the design in correct proportion. Behind the massive brick wall, amazing things have taken place. The old porch has moved forward to become the new living room. The space remaining between the new living room and entry has been converted into a walled garden visible from the living room and sitting room (the old living room). The library is on the right. This addition was architect-designed.

Before the remodeling, this is what the house looked like. Well constructed, it was a sturdy, traditional two-story in a fine neighborhood, close to everything. Buying a new home would have meant giving up a location convenient to work, schools, church, and shopping. Remodeling seemed the best solution. Basically, the family needed more space. A bigger living room, bedrooms, kitchen, and a library that could be used for a guest room. They got them and a new facade.

Inspect your "existing" rooms

As shown in the example on the preceding page, more often than not, the solution to a space problem will be lying right under your nose.

So when inspecting your house, see if you can find (or envision) new uses for those old rooms. And if you find it just too hard to be objective, call in a neighbor or architect for an opinion.

Family rooms

Building an addition has several advantages over moving into a new house. One of them is the knowledge that you have of your present home. Through years of living in your house, you know best where you can improve it.

The addition of a family room is probably one of the most desired home improvements. And most families today consider them almost a necessity for comfortable living. Mothers love them because they can take pressure (and hard wear) from the living room. Family rooms give the youngsters a place to rough-house where the furniture is ready to take it, leaving the living room or dining area free from scrimmage practice.

Generally, it's best to locate a family room near or next to the kitchen. This makes it convenient for serving meals or when entertaining guests. Also, you can keep an eye on the children and the range at the same time. However, if you prefer to have the family room away from the kitchen, go right ahead. Some people would rather have it away from the busy part of the house so they can relax and be informal.

This family-room addition was attached to the kitchen. However, it greatly expanded space in the whole house and not only in one room. Behind the folding louvered screen are the washer and dryer plus a sink and a countertop for folding clothes. This means the laundry equipment is close to the kitchen where the wife can keep her eye on the stove, laundry, and the younger members of her family all at the same time. The table next to the windows makes an informal place to serve meals; since the addition is right next to the kitchen, it is a handy place, as well. And it takes the daily wear from the dining room, since there is no eating area in this kitchen. The family room also expands the kitchen in another way. A barbecue is one of the assets of the room. Now barbecues are possible at any season. Also, a big fan was installed under the range hood to carry smoke outside when the barecue is used. And for a fine play surface, the heavy-duty round rug tops off the room.

How to design an all-purpose family room

When that new addition you build is a family room, make sure you design it for many functions. It should be able to suit small children, teen-agers or adults.

If you intend to make the room a place for family recreation, include furniture and accessories that different members of the family can use. For example, a small-size pool table, a game table, or a table for Ping-Pong are all good choices. But, remember, any furniture in this room must be able to take abuse. So get strong, serviceable furniture. A plastic-topped table is a good example. This can be used as a writing surface, for snacks and drinks, or for a game of monopoly or a hand of bridge.

A family room also can serve as a quiet room. A place where you can chat with friends, watch television, listen to records, or read a book. Adequate lighting is a must and good storage space to hide records, tapes and games is needed, also.

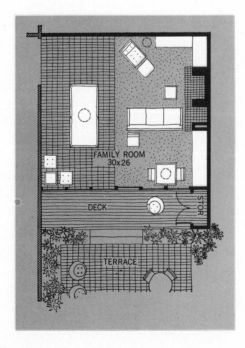

This plan has space for just about any activity you could want. A full-size pool table is incorporated in the design of the room. The table sits on an easy-to-care-for floor that can take the scuffs. The table can also be easily moved aside for dancing, and at Christmas time it can be converted into a handy layout for that new model train. Beyond the table, the floor is carpeted for soundproofing and for comfort underfoot. A game table occupies the space near the windows. It gets good light during the day and has a hanging lamp over it to give the right light during the evening hours. A couch is placed at right angles to the fireplace. It helps to separate the quiet area from the more active parts of the room.

The fireplace claims the center of attention, but it's only one feature of this multi-faceted entertainment room. Bookshelves climb above storage chests. They hold books and accessories above and have room for games and papers below. Beside the storage cupboard is a good location for the television set, where it can be watched from the sofa. On the same side of the room, a chair with a hanging light above it is a fine place to read or to dream while watching the flickering images in the fire. And with a woodbox built in next to the fireplace, you won't have to make trips outdoors.

On the other side of the fireplace, another storage chest has a section that pulls down so you can serve beverages and snacks from it. Extra glasses and bowls can be stored in the cupboards on either side. The top of the cabinet makes a place for suitable accessories. Here, a collection of pottery is given height by the addition of a graceful tree branch; in the winter, you can use an artificial one. One wall is all glass. Sliding glass doors lead to a deck and out onto the terrace. If your view is private, you won't need draperies. A large overhang protects the room from sun and the deck from rain showers. Outdoor plantings dress up the deck and beyond.

This new room has 780 square feet and can be used as an extension of your living room for entertaining. (To obtain construction plans, see pp. 3608-1 in the reference listing.)

Make your family room comfortable

Sometimes entertaining and leisure activity needs are secondary to the need for a place where the family can gather in the evening for conversation and relaxation, and to a spot where the children can loaf before meals— somewhere other than the kitchen.

As mentioned earlier, a family room is best placed near the kitchen. This way it takes the bulk of the traffic away from the other parts of the house. And if your family room is designed primarily for comfort and relaxation, do make sure that the room is outfitted with good comfortable seating for young and old.

How to panel a family room

Many family rooms have wood paneling. It is easy to care for, requires no repainting, and supplies mellow color. Warm wood colors foster a relaxed atmosphere and are a good background for cheery hues.

Paneling also shows off accessories, espe-

This new family room has enough space to seat four school-age children and the parents, too. Twin sofas cluster around an area rug. A large coffee table provides a place to set snacks. The family room is adjacent to the kitchen, and a pass-through is a wise bit of planning. Mom can keep an eye on the activities and supply snacks to starving youngsters, too. Piano practice can also be supervised while dinner is being prepared. The usefulness of the room is not limited to the under-age set. Parties for parents and friends are welcomed here. The pass-through makes it simple to serve refreshments. There's lots of room for gatherings around the piano as well as seating space. The round table hold chips, dips, and dessert plates. The softly gleaming paneling makes the room seem warm and inviting.

cially the soft gleam of metals. Wall decorations that reflect the mood of the room, from any style period, look well. And the best part is that you can do the paneling yourself.

How to liberate your living room

On the whole, most people lean to less than formal entertaining. A room with carefree, rugged materials puts guests at ease, especially when food is served. Then, a spill is no longer a tragedy. The liberation of the living room means children and parents can entertain simultaneously.

How to get more room for entertaining

A family room addition gives you more room—a place for the children to play or to entertain friends without disrupting the rest of the house. And if you attach it to a living room or have it adjoin the kitchen, the results are the same—there's more room for entertaining a large crowd when you want to.

Butternut paneled doors that match the wall paneling conceal a handy storage area in this new family room. Shelves are deep enough to hold even bulky items . Chafing dishes, large platters and trays, plus extra coffee pots fit comfortably on these ample shelves. The rack on the bottom of the closet contains chairs and card tables. It is wise to re-evaluate your storage when you add space. It's always useful.

The family-room addition was added onto the back of this suburban home. It is just two steps below the level of the existing living room. Sliding glass doors lead out to a terrace. The dimensions of the room are 22 × 15½ feet, which yields 340 square feet of floor space. One wall is set aside for storage. An ample cabinet hangs on the wall next to the living room. These storage areas free the rest of the space.

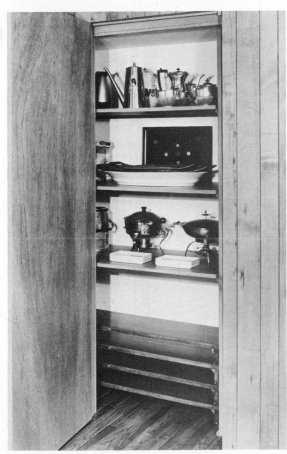

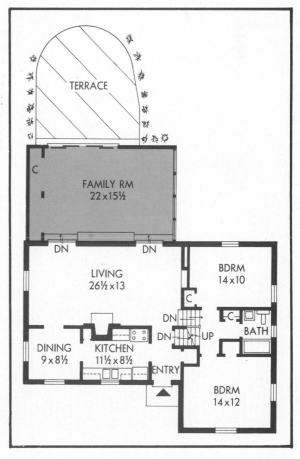

Good planning is the secret behind easy living in family rooms. Plan to leave yourself as much time for fun and relaxation as possible. Take advantage of all the work-saving, low maintenance products, the design ideas of today.

To be truly versatile, a family room should have materials dressy enough for company, yet durable enough for daily use. In other words, you need a family room that actually looks as if it enjoys use—inviting multiple activities of a big and lively group. It should be a room where anything goes. Small children and big dogs can live it up—teen-agers can sprawl, with never a reprimand about wear and tear. Or it can be a place where you can relax and enjoy peace all by yourself.

Here's a truly versatile family room—where anything goes. The colors are warm and friendly. The furniture wood is mellow, durable oak, with some pieces stained to brighten the scene. Painted walls and the beamed ceiling add to cozy informality. Real brick backgrounds coal- and wood-burning Franklin stove. A washable woven-cotton area rug defines conversation area—rolls up for dancing. All upholstery is nylon—spray-protected to withstand constant use.

As seen in the floor plan below, for snacks and parties, refreshments can be passed through from the adjacent kitchen. If it's a big party, the drop-leaf table stretches into a regular-size dining table. The poker table has its own flat-surface cover so it can be pressed into service, too. Either table handles other jobs—sewing, homework, and games. This hospitable room can even double as a guest room. The comfortable sofa accommodates overnight guests.

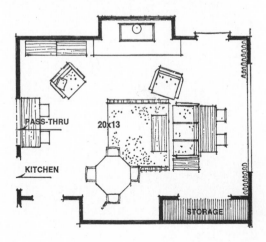

Family rooms for older homes

If you have an older home, don't be terrified by an all-out, stem-to-stern remodeling project. If your house is structurally sound, and in a prime location, a full-scale or even a minor improvement program may yield big dividends. One advantage of remodeling your older home is that with careful planning you can time the work to suit your needs and budget.

And with an older home, one of the best and easiest additions to make is that of a family room. It immediately takes much of the pressure off the rest of the house and at the same time modernizes your home. And the odds are that somewhere in your house, you have the potential for just such a room. Perhaps the space is an attached garage or a corner of the basement. For example, space that's not quite large enough for one of to-day's cars can accommodate a party-full of people, or make roomy, comfortable quarters for family relaxing. And if the spot you choose is completely below ground, you can fake windows by installing lighting behind frosted glass.

When drawing up plans for your family room, be sure to make provisions for adjacent outdoor living. A deck, patio, or porch won't add much to the total cost. And if your budget is really tight, you can put off that part of the job until later—just don't forget to allow for it in the original design.

Here's a perfect example of a family room that was added on to an older home. This multi-purpose room, added to an old section of the house, was designed to integrate dining, living, and kitchen facilities. To combine easy-going living with orderliness, ample storage was a must. Wall-hung cabinets were even placed over the desk at the right of the fireplace. Stained oak beams bring decorative warmth to the textured acoustical ceiling. Rough-sawn cedar paneling covers part of the fireplace wall. Linen-textured vinyl wall covering was used elsewhere. And since the family room was built adjacent to the kitchen, serving meals to the family or refreshments to guests is a cinch.

Living rooms

Is your old living room closing in on you? Need more breathing space? Before you run out and start shopping for a larger house with a larger living room, consider expanding your present one. If your house is basically sound, and you like the neighborhood, the odds are that you will be way ahead by making a major investment right where you are.

When expanding or adding on a new living room, keep in mind the position of your house on the lot and the part that building and zoning regulations will play in where you place your addition. In most cities, there is a limit to how close to your lot line you can build. You may also want to place your new living-room addition so it adjoins a room and permits a natural traffic flow.

Also, if the addition of a living room is to the front of the house, it can change the looks of your entire home. And this gives you a perfect opportunity to change the face of your house; e.g., a new entry way or new building materials or new landscaping can make all the difference in the world.

Generally, the living room is reserved for those formal occasions when you have to entertain. But that doesn't mean it has to have a stuffy look. Keep it and its furnishings casual and comfortable.

Living room with a steeply pitched ceiling is part of a first-floor addition. On the other side of the brick wall is a new study. The addition is a step down from the foyer, which joins the new rooms to the original section of the house. Varicolored crab-orchard stone covers the floor of the foyer. In a corner nook off the living room, a wall cabinet with a marble top contains a bar and storage space. The dining room in the background was the former living room. The wide opening between foyer and dining room is partially screened by decorative metal scrollwork panels that once were gates.

Bedrooms

Remodeling trends indicate the master bedroom is the most drastically changing area of the home. Except for the bed, of course, today's ideal sleeping quarters more closely resemble a well-outfitted second living room.

The multi-purpose master bedroom is no longer an indulgence or a privilege enjoyed by people with space and more to spare. Adults now demand a bedroom retreat as a palliative to fast-paced living. This involves imaginative space-shaping, regardless of the room's size.

Two key factors evolve: space and separation. Consider such things as a sitting area, built-ins for books and hobby equipment, commodious storage, separate dressing-room annex and compartmented bath. Separate your new master-bedroom addition from activity areas that belong in other rooms. Remember, this is a room in which you escape from it all.

To the right, we see the study end of the new master-suite ▶ addition, which includes a dressing room and compartmented bath. Pecky cypress covers the walls, ceiling, and beams. It supplies a natural textured effect and soft, yet light, color. Windows turn the corner to give a wide view. A handsomely carved, king-sized desk faces outward. A lamp tall enough to provide good light for writing adorns one corner. The fireplace is prefabricated. It rests on a geometric, cast-stone base that is just the right size to protect the rug. Next to it, an ornate shelf holds practical accessories such as a lamp and radio, as well as decorative pottery and baskets. Below the shelf are two pillows, covered with a shaggy material and tasseled. They resemble the American Indian rugs that this homeowner collects, and can be used on the bed for reading. A throw made of the same material rests on the bench at the end of the bed.

The dark tones of the furniture contrast with the lighter color of the pecky cypress wall and yellow carpeting. Notice that large surfaces are light. The dark shades are reserved for the furnishings and accessories. Painted woodwork is off-white throughout the whole suite.

Because a kitchen, family room, and bedroom had been added to the house about 15 years ago, there was a flat section of roof that provided the perfect starting place for upward expansion. Now that flat surface is gone from the roof line. It has been transformed into the master suite. The corner windows are the same ones seen in the picture to the right. The addition blends into the existing architecture. A railing around the second floor protects a 3-foot balcony that runs along two sides of the house. The ceiling of the addition follows the roof line. The highest point of the roof makes the division between the bedroom and the dressing room with its compartmented bath. The bath, itself, is divided into sections, allowing more than one person to use the facilities at one time without sacrificing privacy. Because the addition was built on top of the house, the patio in the rear was undisturbed by the project. No new landscaping was needed.

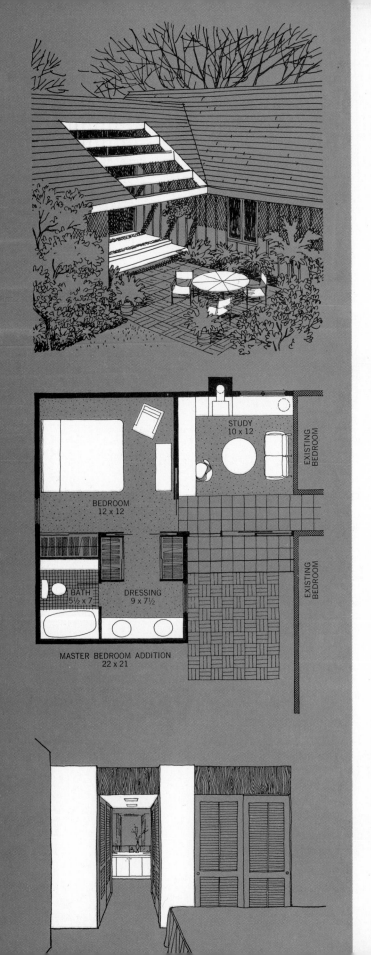

MASTER BEDROOM ADDITION
22 x 21

How to make your bedroom a retreat

Back in the "good old days," bedrooms were more literally bedrooms. People went there when all of the day's activities were finished to seek oblivion until the beginning of the next day's activities.

But now, a master bedroom is more than just a place for sleep; it's a private retreat that should provide enjoyment of every creature comfort. Good sleep equipment, chosen for restfulness and durability, is most important. Then add the convenience of ample storage, an adjoining bath and dressing area.

If you need extra bedroom space, why not consider converting your present bedroom into one for one of the youngsters and building a new bedroom wing with your own bath, study, and sleeping quarters? This kind of plan, upper left drawing, can be attached to many older two- and three-bedroom homes. Simply join it where there's a central hall. It disturbs the rest of the house less if you pick a place where you won't have to create a new corridor. Board-and-batten siding suits many homes. As seen here, the entrance is recessed and the roof left open so that the light can get through.

As you can see, in the second drawing on the left, each of the three rooms is about the same size and is separated by sliding doors. Little furniture is needed in the sleeping area, since you will probably spend most of your waking hours in the study. Clothes are kept in the dressing area. The compartmented bath permits one to bathe while the other washes. The study area can contain a sofa and chair quite easily plus a storage wall with a desk. This arrangement gives privacy to the bath as well as dressing areas.

Three double-door closets, lower left drawing, one in the bedroom and the other two in the hall, guarantee plenty of room for all of your clothes. If you have dressers for your present bedroom furniture, you can put them in one of the closets. You'll still have room to hang shirts and blouses over them. Built-in shelving also supplies space for your needs. You can separate "his" from "hers" or combine areas by size. A 7½-foot-long countertop has twin lavatories. Use the vanity to spread out makeup or shaving gear.

This sketch, to the right, shows one possible decorating ▶ scheme for the entrance and the study area. The wide steps and open roof, in addition to the greenery, provide a transition between the patio and interior. The decorative details of the study depend upon your interests. If you like to sew, you might conceal your sewing equipment here. If you prefer Early American to Contemporary, there's no reason why this room can't be supplied with rustic charm. The window in the study plus the entrance allows for lots of daylight. The dressing area has a dropped luminous-grid system. Planters are used here to line the entrance. (To obtain plans, refer to pp. 3608-11 in the reference listing.)

This new addition, above, can give 132 square feet of multifunctional space to your home. Here it is shown added to the rear of a house, near the other bedrooms. As an added attraction, a circular patio was built around a tree in back of the addition. It is a most impressive gambit to please your guests; and it can even be used by the rest of the family during their "drop-in" visits.

When you are looking for a place to add this room, it would be best to consider connecting it where it is convenient to the main living areas and close to a bath that guests can have all to themselves. It can be placed on any side of the house—but, generally, the rear of the home is preferable. This is truly a multi-purpose bedroom. It can be used three ways: as a bedroom, as a guest room, and as an office.

The arrangement of this room looks deceptively simple. Actually, it is planned to make the most use of the space available. A sofa to the right of the coffee tables opens right up into a bed for visiting house guests. Those mar-resistant coffee tables double as suitcase racks when necessary. And when the bed is opened, guests are still able to sit on the two chairs to put their shoes on or just to relax.

Storage space surrounds the desk. Books and magazines are always a welcome find to guests who may like to read before they go to sleep. There's plenty of room for light or heavy reading plus a handy desk for writing. Another good idea is to leave a good supply of stationery out for visiting guests.

How to add an office-guest bedroom

Now you can have two rooms in one simply by adding on a new office-guest bedroom. And when a new room addition can perform two jobs, it's even more desirable.

First of all, the room can serve as a place to study, work or just plain relax. Secondly, you have a perfect spot to put up guests when they drop in. Place the addition near a bath, or add a new one, and you have the perfect retreat—for either you or your guests.

Such an addition will look well anywhere, but preferably it should be away from the main flow of traffic. Remember, it's a place for you to work and for guests to relax and to sleep. And, if possible, plan to build a patio adjoining the new addition. This gives added "breathing" space and provides indoor-outdoor living for you and your guests.

One of the most crucial purchases for this room will be the sleeper sofa. It's best to buy a large one so that it can sleep at least two people comfortably, and also supply ample seating for your family or for your guests. Besides the sofa, of course, you will need a desk, chairs and ample storage space. A telephone extension is important for this room and an outside exit is convenient. You won't have to wait up, and guests can come and go as they please.

Late nights at the office are a thing of the past when you have ▶ this versatile room addition. Now you can come home, enjoy a good dinner, and finish the job in your own private executive suite. The cabinets below will centralize all your household bills and papers, as well as house a stereo and a portable television. Reserve part of the space for storing the pillows and linens for the sofa bed.

The shelves of the built-in storage wall adjust easily to hold different-size books and accessories. A dimming switch controls the low-voltage lights that are recessed in the ceiling. Only the coffee tables need to be moved to provide space for opening the sofa bed for overnight guests. The tables beside the sofa make perfect nightstands. Their plastic tops take almost any kind of punishment. (To obtain plans for this addition, refer to pp. 3608-7 in the reference listing.)

The pass-through space at the end of the kitchen allows you to peer into the new dining area, which was formerly the old kitchen. It is on the left, while to the right is a game area in the space that was the former dining room.

The addition has opened up these areas of the house, making them all seem larger. You can also see the planning center with lots of storage. Here's the place for your telephone, close to where you keep your records. Things you don't use often can go on the top shelves. The laundry room is half hidden behind the louvered door. It can be closed off completely when not in use.

The efficiency of the addition is matched by the functional architecture, a modified contemporary styling that harmonizes with many kinds of homes. The wall of glass and the redwood cathedral ceiling make the new kitchen addition look both handsome and spacious. You feel you're outdoors while still inside. Sliding glass doors lead out onto the deck. All-weather chairs and table are prepared for instant picnics and hard use. It's a good place to serve the youngsters afternoon treats in the summer. Patio plantings bring the yard up to the kitchen door. (To obtain the plan for this kitchen addition, refer to pp. 3608-13 in the reference listing.)

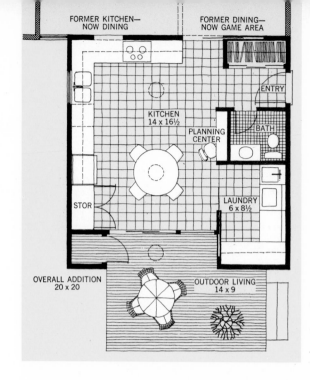

This kitchen addition in the plan pictured to the right has enough space for many functions. The areas are organized to save steps, and there's room for chairs and a generous table. Clockwise from the table are a double-door pantry, refrigerator, mixing center, sink, and cooking center. A planning center includes storage space for cookbooks and household files. The laundry center has space for washer and dryer and a countertop that takes some of the work from the folding chore. Outside the kitchen windows, a deck provides a pleasant view as well as space for meals in the fresh air. You can tell from this tour just how much convenience is here.

Kitchens

With imagination and daring, you can make your new kitchen addition the most unusual and decorative room in the house. And it need not be large to be efficient. A compact, well-designed kitchen minimizes leg work, lets everything flow from it. In planning a new kitchen, it's a good idea to include these ten basics that add to the overall efficiency:

(1) Plan for a breakfast bar or eating area. The only acceptable alternate is to see that service can really be quick to an adjacent dining room.

(2) Organize for good traffic patterns. Provide easy access to an outdoor eating area, the front entry hall, the dining room and a bath.

(3) Choose appliances scaled to the size of the room. Select a compact range for a kitchen short on work counters. For double-oven convenience in the same space, consider a range styled with an oven above and below the cook-top—provided there's ample storage elsewhere.

(4) Allow one generous work counter at least 2 feet wide and 4 feet long for pastry making and party preparation (e.g., mixing drinks or fixing snacks).

(5) Storage that's convenient and space-saving is a must. This means adjustable shelves, easy-operating drawers with dividers, pull-out shelves in the deep storage units to avoid long reaches.

(6) Consider a floor-to-ceiling pantry to keep vast quantities of food or dishes on shallow, easy-to-find shelves.

(7) A great cleanup center including the sink, dishwasher, disposer, mixer faucets, waste paper, can and bottle receptacles, paper-towel dispenser, can opener, hardwood cutting board is a real plus.

(8) Plan on lots of light. Extra-large windows for natural light. A high-wattage central fixture controlled by a dimmer dial. Individual lights above sink, appliances, and work tops are also needed.

(9) Add many electrical outlets so you can plug in small appliances at each work center—and at the table, too.

(10) Include good ventilation. An exhaust fan above the cook-top with easy-to-clean filters keeps grease off of cabinets and walls. And don't rush, take your time.

A fifty-year-old house that was completely remodeled now boasts this exciting new kitchen. Notice its unusual combination of textures and materials. The warm tones of mustard yellow wall cabinets and base units in marigold and orange show to beautiful advantage against the rough-sawn cedar walls and the rich color of the antiqued glazed tile from Japan that's used on the backsplash. And the kitchen is also set up for maximum efficiency. The stainless steel sink won't chip like porcelain, is easy to keep clean, withstands rugged use, and will virtually last a lifetime. There's plenty of storage space both above and below. The counter top is ideal for preparing foods. Automatic dishwasher gets rid of thankless job.

The 12 × 10-foot kitchen looks larger than it really is, possibly because of the feeling of space that's provided by a 9-foot-high ceiling—now treated to acoustical tile and modular lighting panels. Contemporary dining grouping in the spacious eating area is used side by side with choice antiques that furnish wall space just to the right of the table. The rough-sawn cedar is continued on the walls in the dining area, with yellow shutters on the windows for contrast and to carry over the color scheme in the kitchen. Range hood over the oven keeps exhaust and smoke from hanging in the kitchen or drifting over to the dining area. Also, a handy serving counter top is next to the stove, which saves unnecessary steps.

A fanciful ceiling treatment sets the decorative scheme in this handsome kitchen addition. A carved figurehead, resembling those used on Viking ships, is backed up by ash wood curved and shaped like the keel and ribs of a ship. Between the ribs, Thai silk, broad striped in citron and avocado, covers the ceiling and extends down to the tops of the wall cabinets. Curves on the door fronts repeat the lines of the ceiling ribs. Again this kitchen is designed for maximum efficiency. Plenty of storage cabinets above and below the sink. Counter-top space makes preparing and mixing foods a real cinch. And the automatic dishwasher makes cleaning dishes almost fun.

The decorative scheme started in the kitchen is effectively carried over to the dining area. The rustic chandelier and heavy-looking wood chairs and table add emphasis to the Viking theme. Also, Thai silk wall covering is reemphasized in the informal dining area. The modern clock on the wall, the unusual glass design on the door, and the modern appliances contrast beautifully with the rustic theme. Range hood over the stove helps keep walls and cabinets clean—and the heat out of the kitchen and dining area. Notice the large amount of counter space next to the range—makes it easier for Mom to prepare foods or to set hot dishes down before serving.

Patios

A patio is one addition that you can build yourself. It's relatively easy and inexpensive. For example, ordinary concrete makes one of the most versatile of patio materials. It fills depressions, flows around rocks, and makes an unlimited number of two-dimensional shapes. All you have to do is contain its horizontal

Here's a simple but decorative patio. Smooth white concrete on this patio (right) contrasts with a massive black divider grid made up of old railroad ties treated with a black preservative stain. That rectangle in the foreground is a planter with white gravel mulch. When pouring the cement in this type of grid effect, fill every other form. This way you can work on all four sides of each of the squares. Screening and surfacing will be much easier and will go faster.

This patio extends from the family' room, making indoor-outdoor living a pleasure. The patio is large enough so that a large group can sit out there comfortably having a picnic or while talking and admiring the beautiful garden surrounding it. The surface of the patio consists of blocks with exposed-aggregate finish. The finish is made by spreading smooth pebbles on top of poured concrete, tamping in place, and troweling the surface. A curing agent is then applied.

flow and provide level surfaces from which you can screen away excess material. Any shape that stops the flow will be reproduced.

You can also build with concrete by forming it into individual paving blocks. You can mass-produce them in your back yard, then lay them one at a time on a sand base. Whether you work with large areas or a piece at a time, you can choose from a wide variety of concrete surface textures and designs.

Exposed-aggregate concrete (below) is one of the most popular types of surface finish. Here, the concrete is poured in a grid of redwood 2 × 4's, smooth pebbles are spread on top and tamped in place, and the surface is troweled. Then a chemical curing agent is applied and surface mortar cleaned from the tops of pebbles. A fence around the patio assures privacy for the homeowners. The furniture used for the patio is decorative, rugged—and replaceable, if necessary.

This is the way the house looked before the patio and carport were built. The barbecue which was installed where the owners requested it can be seen at the left side of the chimney stack. The homeowners had decided to build a full garage and a patio while the house was still in the blueprint stage. They knew they wanted a patio, but decided to wait.

They wanted to live in the house for a while before making any definite plans for adding on to the house. They reasoned that this would enable them to learn the good and the bad points of the house and what was needed.

The house was near a large tree, which would provide protection to the patio. They positioned the garage so that, in combination with the storage wall, it would give shelter on three sides of the patio. The fourth side was left open.

The carport was eventually built where the homeowners specified. As seen in the plan below, they then had it converted into a full garage with a storage and work area. The patio was constructed behind the garage with room left beside it to give entry into the house.

Now the outside wall of the garage extends to the end of the patio. Another storage cupboard at the farthest end of the wall holds supplies for the patio. One section of the patio wall is louvered to let some breeze blow through. The floor of the patio is made of concrete rectangles divided by redwood strips. Some areas of the floor are left open, so the homeowners can plant flowers near the fence. Other planted areas next to the house and in the entry between the garage and the house.

How to plan your patio

With the emphasis on outdoor living, no home landscape is complete without an outdoor living area—a patio. And probably the two most important rules for planning your patio are to make it big enough, and as private as you can. Its accessibility is nearly as important—the more parts of your house that open onto it, the more enjoyment your family will derive from it. Another thing to keep in mind is that relaxation is the whole point of any patio, so plan yours with low maintenance foremost in your mind. A major planning

This is the result of careful planning and waiting. The outdoor living area is close to the kitchen so picnics are easily served, and children can be watched, too. The lattice-work covering on the patio permits daylight to come through, but it takes the sting from the sun's hottest rays. Overhead beams extend from the garage roof and fit snugly against the house. The beams unite the garage and house, making them look as though they are a part of one unit instead of two separate sections. The extension of the garage wall also provides the patio and the living room windows with a privacy fence. Tender plants that need protection can grow in this sheltered location. The view from the living room is onto the planted section of the patio. The big tree adds further shade.

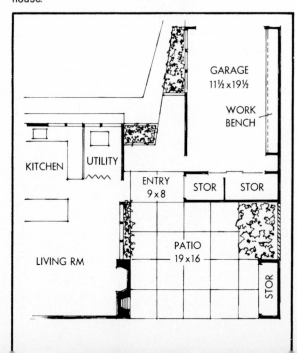

consideration to take into account is the exact function you intend for your patio. Is it going to be used primarily for outdoor cooking and entertaining? If so, then you should include a barbecue of some sort. Or is the patio only to be a nice cozy nook where you can relax, get some fresh air and escape from the hustle-bustle of everyday living? If so, then plan your patio accordingly.

Where to place your patio

More often than not, the exact location of the contemplated patio will be determined by the placement of the house on the lot. Taking this into account, next you must see if you can connect this outdoor addition with an entrance to the house. This is especially helpful if the patio is to be used for outdoor dining. Two excellent places to build your new patio are either off the kitchen or off the family room. Both make it convenient for indoor-outdoor pleasure at a mere opening of a door, and both are ideal if you plan to entertain, be it barbecuing or for just chatting.

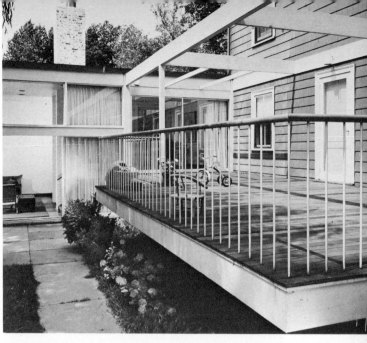

This outdoor deck does more than provide space for outdoor leisure activities. It is a design feature that functions as a transitional member between the modern lines of the new living wing and the traditional two-story home. It helps blend the two diverse styles into one unified structure. The dropped living room and the overhang on the deck-patio also serve to support the combination of the two styles and merge the two structures with the surrounding land. The deck is 3½ feet above ground level. It and its overhang carry the eye from the straight lines of the new addition over to the older part. Out of sight, at the right, are wooden steps which lead from the deck into the yard. Next to the deck, concrete squares form a small courtyard. A privacy fence shelters it from the street.

The before plan shows the original use of space. It also points out the fairly limited amount of room in the home before the addition. The house was, however, set back on a narrow lot. When the architect studied the house and the lot, he adapted his design to fit the available space. The results were unusual and drastic, satisfying and useful in bringing space and utility to an old and plain house. This project shows the forethought on the part of the owners in hiring an architect to help them. Their investment paid off in the production of a unique design and the wise use of space.

The new living arrangement makes the best use of the long narrow lot as well as satisfying the family's requirements. The front entrance is now closer to the street while the portions that require quiet are more remote. An intercom system links different parts of the house. The new kitchen was placed between the dining room and the family room. Off the family room we have the deck-patio. The living room is a few steps below the dining area. The new entry has room for a half bath as well as storage closets.

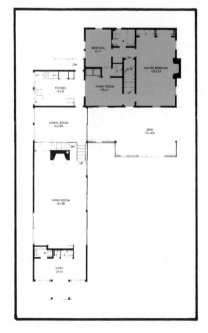

How to decide on the size of your patio

When trying to determine exactly what size you would like your new patio to be, try to think of it as another room of the house. It will have to be furnished and decorated using an approach similar to that applied to any room in the house. Don't forget that it will probably have some permanent fixtures and a definite function. However, unlike an existing interior room, you do have some control over its size and location. If you plan to use your patio mainly for barbecuing and dining, better make it a fairly good size. On the other hand, if it's going to be a restful place for you to get away from it all, it won't have to be quite so large.

A good way to help you arrive at the correct size is for you to try to visualize the furnishings and barbecue—if you intend to have one. In the same manner as when you are arranging or decorating an inside room, set up a floor arrangement plan. You might use cardboard boxes to represent furnishings on the patio site.

And also, while discussing the idea of a barbecue, make sure that you check the prevailing breezes on the selected patio site— before you install a permanent barbecue fix-

This backyard patio-pavilion has two rooms and a screened entry from the house. The room in the foreground has a solid roof so you can stay here even when the rain falls. The section beyond, which includes the table and chairs, has an open roof that is screened to keep the bugs out. Here, you can get your ration of sunshine. The roofed section also contains a storage cabinet for gardening tools and patio furniture. The patio-pavilion is built of 4 × 4- and 2 × 4-inch lumber. Two 4 × 10-inch beams run the entire length. Solid panels are combined with the screening to give extra strength and block breezes. To let light through, you can use colorful plastic panels. Plantings in the yard continue uninterruptedly into the pavilion area. (To obtain plans for this patio-pavilion refer to PP. 3608-8 in your plans reference listing.)

This patio-deck is L-shaped so that it wraps around the house. The sketch above shows the deck adjoining the dining room. Sliding glass doors make exit and entry easy. A dining table is placed near the doors so food does not have to be carried far. The plantings shown in the plan are merely accessories. The seating area is beyond the dining room. A door from another room in the house—could be kitchen, bedroom or living room—leads onto the seating area.

ture. All too often, people have discovered, much to their dismay after finishing the job, that the wind drifts all the barbecue smoke from the fire into the sitting area. Naturally, this can be more than just a little bit annoying—not only to you but more especially to your guests.

The patio-deck pictured below is raised off the ground so that it is on the same level as the floor of the house. The railing around three sides of the deck doubles as a bench, thus providing lots of seating space. Partial shade is supplied by the open-beam roof. And for nighttime illumination, floodlights can be attached. This patio-deck furnishes 288 square feet of extra living space. That's plenty of room for several tables of bridge or a child's birthday party. If you build a terrace beyond the patio, you can have even more space for entertaining. Plantings around the deck can hide the foundation. If you do not have trees, plant a few where they'll give protection from the afternoon sun. You can accessorize the patio by using colorful tubs filled with tall plants. Use varieties you can bring indoors in the winter, or buy realistic-looking artificial plants. If you don't bring the plants inside in the winter, use false greenery for contrast when it snows.

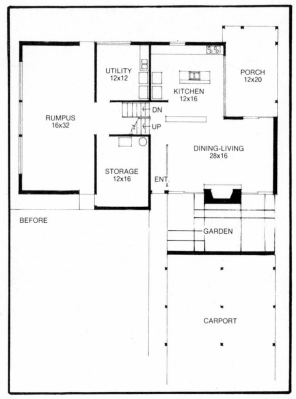

BEFORE

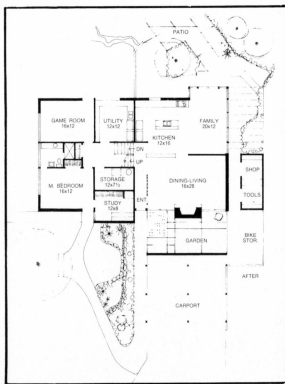

AFTER

This is the floor plan before the house was remodeled. When the architect-owner originally built his home, small children in the family called for a close relationship between parents' and children's bedrooms. Also at this time, the family needed less space for outdoor activities. However, as the children became teen-agers—more space became necessary.

Here's the new floor plan (lower left) after the house was redesigned and space re-utilized. Notice how many new additions were added: a large patio, workshop, shed for garden tools, family room (once the old porch), game room, master bedroom with bath, a study, and even a storage shed for bikes. And to set the new additions off, extensive landscaping was done.

How to achieve extra comfort

Pulling out a couple of folding chairs to enjoy a summer evening is rapidly becoming a thing of the past. Today, it's more common to find a permanent outdoor living area that is protected from wind and wet grounds. Wood-floor patios, screened-in concrete areas, and decks are but a few of the many different ideas that suburbanites consider necessities. Not only do they provide comfort, but they are profitable to incorporate, too.

How to increase the value of your home

Building an outdoor living area can be a good investment. A carefully planned outdoor patio with landscaping can boost the resale value of your home by much more than what the improvement costs you.

A landscape architect can design a plan for your particular lot, one that not only enhances the looks of your house but also your yard. The biggest expense is, of course, labor. And this is where you can save yourself some money—by doing the work yourself, just a little at a time.

Finishing touches

To keep weeds and grass from growing between concrete blocks or patio wood floors, treat the area with a general or non-selective weed killer. One application is about all that is needed to last a full season. Low walls can be added at patio boundaries and planted with either annuals or perennials. Roses are always a favorite choice. Add several trees to furnish a roof for shade in locations where the sun shines hot for long hours. Since it will take time for trees to grow, a temporary cover may be needed. A constructed roof or awning is easily installed. Next, add what personal touches you like. Then go out and enjoy your patio—you'll find there's nothing like it.

The swing sets and sandboxes in the backyard, installed when the children were young, have been replaced by this attractive, free-form patio, complete with benches and table. Now the outside area serves both the older and the younger generation. Brick steps and landings lead up from the family-room level to the patio's concrete aggregate surface—a natural place for guests to "overflow to" from the family room.

Shown below is an exterior view of the new family room. Surrounded with glass, guests and family are afforded an exquisite view of the patio and landscape. A trellis-covered walkway leads to some other outdoor changes. These include a shed for a workshop and garden tool storage, plus an enclosure for out-of-sight bicycle storage. The architect-owner combined outdoor-indoor living in the very truest sense.

A screened porch now has walls of glass. The wall separating it from the kitchen was removed; sliding glass doors formerly connecting the living area to the porch were sealed off; and the new family room emerged. To finish it off, polished slate flooring, easy-to-clean furnishings, and an acoustical ceiling were installed.

How To Achieve Comfort Control Without Breaking Your Budget

Comfort control in the home is possible with year-round air conditioning, whether you have an older home or a newer one, which can take a sophisticated system. The only difficulty lies in deciding what type of air conditioning unit to buy. To a large extent, this will depend upon what kind of heating unit, if any, you have.

Types of air conditioners

If your home is heated with forced air, you already have part of your job done—the ducts will serve both the heating and the cooling systems. It is a very simple matter for a contractor to hook up the additional system. But do watch out that your ducts project upward. This is necessary to insure forcing cooling air throughout the home.

On the other hand, if your unit is part of a split system with the condenser-compressor located outdoors on a concrete slab, you may have to contract for the installation of a duct system. This is often the case with older homes. But, again, if you have a central heating unit, there is no difficulty. Then the inside evaporator coil will be located between the warm-air furnace blower and the ducts.

If your home doesn't have a forced-air system and relies on a hot-water heating unit, you should investigate using a hydronic system. This sends cooled water through the pipes during the warm, humid summer months. Fan-coil units—blowers which move air over the chilled coils—or radiators distribute the cool air and allow temperature control

in each room. This is, however, the most expensive system.

Yet another way, and one which is fast growing in popularity, involves the use of a heat pump. This unit provides year-round comfort control. It heats the house during the winter months, and reverses the process in summer. These pumps, which are maintained outside the house, are efficient, clean, and installed economically. (If the condensing unit is to be outdoors, make certain it's not under a bedroom window because of on-off noises.)

The last method involves the time-honored window unit. Here a unit which is easily installed is fitted into the window. It can be run by either gas or electricity, and can also be water cooled. This latter condition is usually reserved for areas of little humidity.

Buy a system not a unit

Besides the obvious answer that an air conditioning system will cool your home, it is also a home improvement with a built-in safeguard. It won't depreciate like most other household items. If you sell your home, you get back a larger percentage of the original cost of your unit than with any other home improvement project.

You'll have fewer worries all summer long, too. You can leave your house locked up all day, and yet it won't be hot and stuffy when you return at night. This, in turn, means that you can safeguard against prowlers. That little crack you left at the top of the window to allow some cool air in needn't be left open any more.

When to buy an air conditioning system

Early spring, late autumn, and winter are the best times to purchase an air conditioning system. For one thing, these are the times when you are most likely to get a price reduction on the equipment. Manufacturers must keep their product-lines busy, and the same holds for retailers. Air conditioning contractors, too, are looking for work. They prefer to space their work-load year-round, thus avoiding the summer peaks. If anything, at these times of the year, they are often inclined to reduce their price.

The above conditions, too, apply to the purchase of a window unit.

How to choose the right contractor

Select two contractors and ask them to submit bids. They will look over your house, establish the equipment you need, and then talk about price. Listen, ask questions, but don't necessarily go for the low bid. Look over the estimate thoroughly.

Has the contractor taken your needs into consideration? If your home is small and short on space, has he suggested a split system—moving part of the equipment out of the house? Check to see if he has taken the cost of utilities into consideration. Generally, the installation of a gas-powered system is high and the maintenance costs are relatively low. Ask if the equipment is certified by the Air Conditioning and Refrigeration Institute. If it is, check the rating. Then weigh the warranties offered by each contractor. Once all these facts are in you may realize that the low bid wasn't the best, after all.

Once you've made your choice, ask the contractor for a written contract spelling out the details of the work to be done, the equipment selected, and a schedule for the installation. Then push a button marked "on."

An air conditioning unit in a window is not the easiest thing in the world to include in a decorating scheme. Here's one way to make it look like a planned part of the room. Make it seem as if it were an architectural feature that provides some extra storage space, too. It's not a difficult project.

First, you need to build a framework of lumber, fastened to the wall with cleats. Next install the air conditioner in the window. Now add the shelves. Then attach louvered shutters, which are pre-hinged to the frames.

In this arrangement the inside of the middle shelf was painted to match the color of the air conditioner. The shelf repeats the color of the walls and shutters. If you make the storage unit the same color as the wall, it makes an unbroken surface of color across the wall. If you wanted to accent the storage unit, you might paint it white or another color to contrast with the shade of the wall.

In this kind of arrangement, you can hide the air conditioner when it is not in use. Just close the shutter doors.

How to care for air conditioners

Once your air conditioning unit is installed, there are one or two things you can do to improve its continued efficiency.

One way is to keep the unit clean. Check filters regularly to make certain they are clean. When necessary, replace them. Do the same with feed lines.

Another way is to cut down on the amount of heat you allow to enter your home. Screen your house against the sun's rays by planting trees and shrubs before open spaces. And in the heat of the day keep the draperies drawn across those windows where the sun enters.

Inside the house, check to be sure that your insulation is adequate. You need three inches in the wall, four to six inches in the roof.

Remember, air conditioning does more than cool your home. It also filters and dehumidifies the air. Greater comfort and health benefits are realized as a result. For truly effective climate control—and for economic efficiency—the basic rule is: when you turn on your air conditioning unit, leave it on.

This alcove has a dual function. It serves as a storage area, and as a convenient niche to house the air conditioning unit. In each case, it's in easy reach, but high enough to be out of the way, and makes the most economical use of the space.

The near-ceiling position is financially economic, too. Cool air falls, so you get better cooling with this high position for the air conditioning unit, and it lightens your utility bill.

Extra storage space is always welcome. There's plenty of attractive space for books or knickknacks in this curved alcove. The shelves are deep enough that they will take the widest book. And this depth also allows using the area in front of the air conditioning unit as additional storage space in winter when the unit is not used.

Hinged shutters are a versatile way to disguise an air conditioning unit. They can be adapted to fit any room style, and can be made from different materials. In this one, the inside of the panels has been covered with shirred fabric.

Other decorative panels can also be used. Instead of fabric, you can use wood, translucent plastic that looks like patterned or colored glass, cane, or ornamental wire mesh. Whatever your choice of material, you can paint or color it to blend or contrast with your walls or furnishings.

This is one way to bring your air conditioner into the room's color scheme. The fabric can be material left over from another room project. In this way you integrate the unit into your color scheme *and* your decorating scheme.

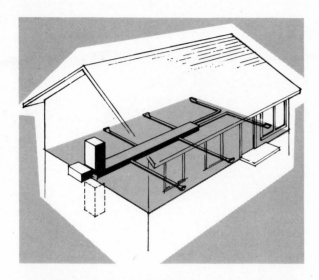

If you don't have room in the attic and if you have no basement, this floor air supply may be what you need. A compact down-flow unit fits in a hall closet. If you have a basement, then you can install the cooling unit to operate through the furnace. Since registers at floor level are used, you may need to increase the size of the blower unit. Because cool air drops and hot air rises, registers that are efficient for heating may be less so when they are used for cooling.

You help any kind of duct system by setting the blower so it runs constantly, not just during the cooling cycle. With CAC (Continuous Air Circulation) your system doesn't have to work quite so hard because the blower keeps the cool air circulating evenly throughout the house. The air is prevented from settling in a chilly layer at floor level. It is cleaner, too, because it is sent through the filter more often.

Place the thermostat in the most important room on an inside wall, away from direct sunlight or sources of indoor heat.

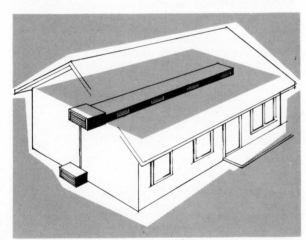

The hallway supply-system is one of the simplest ones. A single self-contained air conditioner, which includes all the components—cooling coil, compressor, condenser, and fans—is mounted at ceiling height. It projects through an outside wall so the condenser end of the cooler can release heat to the outside air. Inside, a long plenum (a sheet metal duct that is the same size from one end to the other) runs from the air conditioner to the farthest end of the house. You can run it along a central bedroom hall or go directly through a series of parallel walls.

Cool air registers in the sides of the duct provide cool air to the rooms it passes through, and short ducts supply registers in other rooms. Warm air enters the cooler directly since there are no warm air return registers. Air movement, however, is at ceiling height so there are no direct drafts.

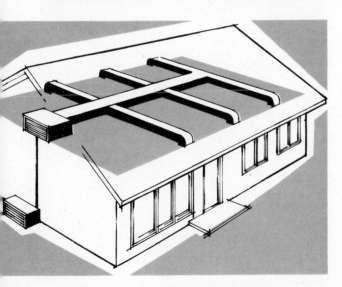

If you decide that the attic is the best place for some or all of your air conditioning equipment, you need to make a few preparations for it. Build platforms where they are needed with a catwalk between them and the stairs or trapdoor. You also need to make sure that the attic supports are strong enough to bear the weight. Self-contained conditioners are especially heavy and you may discover you need extra support.

If your house doesn't have a central-hall plan or you don't want the ducting to show, you can use this attic supply system. The condenser extends through the wall. You may need a bracket outdoors for extra support. Two plenums are attached to the air conditioner, a short one for returning warm air, and a long one for cool air. The short warm air plenum leads to a large, centrally located register. The cool air plenum is connected to smaller registers in .each room by well insulated sheet metal pipes. Insulating the pipes and the plenums is important so they don't soak up heat from the attic air.

This system is quieter than the ceiling duct one, but noisier than furnace-connected air conditioners. A remote type of attic unit is practically silent. This system is actually two separate pieces of equipment with connecting refrigerant lines. The compressor and condenser are outside; inside at the center of the attic is the fan and cooling coil. Two short plenums come from each end. One is the return air duct, and the other supplies cool air to registers in the rooms.

How To Use Small Areas In A Dozen Exciting New Ways

Alcoves are the recesses and niches, which are found in homes, that seem to be tucked away. Windows are often set off in them; hallways may become them; and they may form the depth for a bookcase or knick-knack rack beside a fireplace. Modern homes generally shy away from alcoves.

It seems these recesses were first introduced in Roman homes, as small, intimate bedrooms—a room set off from a larger room. The idea was continued through the Middle Ages when small rooms were set off from the main areas of congregation as bedrooms. While they were separate rooms they were still a part of the main room. The idea continued into late periods, and as recently as the 18th century special beds were made to fit into bedroom alcoves.

But alcoves were not only used for bedrooms. In Elizabethan times alcoves were used to house dining groups, as window seats, or popularly as music rooms. And in Mediterranean areas, alcoves were designated as areas for housing statues, or small, stone love seats. In Spain often they were set off by a partition of columns.

Today, there are myriad uses for an alcove. Depending on the decorating style of the house, an alcove can serve as an area for a bookcase, a cabinet, a vanity or small dressing table, or a niche for a statue or a love seat. If the recessed area is large, it can be used as a dining room, a piano or music room, or a small-sized bedroom. Whatever the size, an alcove should not be wasted space.

How to change an alcove into a vanity

The "ugly" window dormer can make a charming vanity if you tackle the job in the right frame of mind. Make it personal by setting it off from the rest of the bedroom. Give the vanity a different color, though keeping it related to the color scheme of the bedroom; and use it to give the master bedroom a greater touch of femininity.

Place mirrors on the side walls and have a square mirror in front of you. Or, if you can afford the loss of natural light, brick in the area and insert a full-window mirror. Then conceal strip lighting overhead and alongside the mirror. The only other additions you need are a table-top, small drawer-space, and a chair—which should be used as the connecter, pulling the vanity into the decorating scheme.

This desk doubles as a bedroom dressing table. It is built between two closets and allows the window to supply needed light and ventilation. The whole setting is given a touch of elegance by the addition of the red and blue Austrian shade and an ornate chandelier. A few accessories on the table top bring the color down from the shade and provide storage for jewelry and cosmetics. The drawers hold what the top won't—paper, pencils, and stationery, or gloves and scarves.

If you have a window niche in your bedroom, you can duplicate this desk for about $20. The cost depends on the size of the alcove and how much material you need. If it's about the same size as this one, you can make the whole thing from one sheet of ¾-inch plywood and a few pieces of hardboard for drawer bottoms. The center section lifts up and is mirrored. Make the drawer unit first. It should be a little smaller than the niche so it can slip into place easily. Then attach it to the wall and conceal the crack on either side with molding. Cut table top to exact size, then cut out and hinge the mirrored section. This desk was painted white, and antiqued.

How to discover new uses for old closets

Old closets, too, make ideal alcoves. All you need is a hammer to pull out the old nails, and the imagination to dream up ideas for using your closet for a more decorative, though functional, purpose.

You can build in a desk with shelves to store dictionaries or reference books, such as encyclopedias: Or turn the old space into record shelves—to store hundreds of albums and single records. These shelves are ideal for housing the stereo system, and are conveniently placed.

Collectors, too, find many uses for recessed areas. Dishes, shells, antiques, and trophies are suitable for display in an alcove. These areas can also be used as photographic galleries to display the whole family.

If the once-closet now-alcove is in the family room, you can turn it into a small piano room. This is an excellent use of an area in a house with growing children. The piano is there where it is needed, and when practice is over sliding doors can close up the area—when this is desired.

Don't let the size of the closet bother you. You can even pretty it up and turn it into a teen-ager's phone booth.

An organ or a piano is sometimes a difficult piece of furniture to fit into a room arrangement. Fitting it into an unused closet is an ideal way of solving the problem. Here a wide, shallow closet was eliminated to make a piano alcove. This type of treatment also allows you to build a series of shelves, which can hold music and hobby equipment, from 2 × 2-foot stud-wall partitions. The light at one end of the piano lights the music and also shines into the shelving area.

A double closet that was removed provides a showcase for the many uses to which you can put an alcove. Shelves are spaced for books above louvered doors, which conceal guest-room storage space. The doors also swing open to allow room for the guest to sit before a small desk.

The unit was made quite simply. The louvered doors were attached to a frame that had a shelf on top. And the book shelves were placed on self brackets.

In this den there was no place for a buffet or bar. Some quick thinking, a few dollars of material, and this small alcove became an exotic reminder of tropical vacations.

The tropical atmosphere was easy to establish. The bamboo was created by *trompe l'oeil* wallpaper. And a further hint of the outdoors was provided by the ivy that hangs on the wall. A bamboo table, two small fish prints, and this alcove became a tropical welcome wagon.

This Victorian bedroom needed a lift. What was once a closet was turned into a curio-wall that added individuality to the room. The material cost was minimal, but the total effect is majestic.

To provide contrast with the lines of the Victorian furniture and wallpaper, a dark wallpaper backs this alcove. Then four shelves were suspended on wall brackets. The small objects on the shelves help to provide the lift for this room.

How to make the best use of small rooms

There are many uses for the small room which is set off by a divider or by a door. While still part of the main area, this room-size alcove can be transformed into a dining room, music room, bedroom, or conversational area.

If it is close by the kitchen, turn it into a breakfast or coffee room. Clear the room of unwanted cupboards and shelves and make it sprightly. Your objective is to provide yourself with a room that by its mood sets the pattern for the day.

Hang menus on the walls. Select recipes that are family favorites, from your favorite cookbook, and those that have been handed down from daughter to daughter; mount them on a board. A clear lacquer applied over the surface antiques the recipes.

Put down an all-weather carpet or some form of tile on the floor. As this is a casual family room, you need not worry if growing children spill food on the floor.

When these rooms are close by the family room they make ideal music rooms. Again you should let the room assume the atmosphere of a music room. Take out unnecessary articles; put in piano or other instruments. You might hang photographs of musicians or composers on the walls. You might even hang a copy of music scales, mounted on board.

Another excellent idea for a room-size alcove is to turn it into a guest bedroom. If you place in the room a phonograph and a small bookcase, this room can also be used as an occasional room during the day.

And in a small home or apartment the room-size alcove can be a heaven-sent area, shut off for a teen-ager's retreat.

How to make full use of hallways

A hallway or entryway is an alcove, but all too often its space is wasted. By careful thought, and with little cost, you can turn these drab areas into sparkling alcoves.

This is the area your guests see first, so decorate it with bold, bright colors. In this way, the guest's first impression of your home will be a good one.

But this is not only an area for greetings and goodbyes. It is also a storage area. If there is a cupboard, make it attractive. Keep it clean, and make sure there are hangers available and a rack for wet shoes. If there is not a cupboard, install an eye-level hanger. This can be in wood that matches the mood of your entryway. Try an antique wood clothes hanger if your walls are wood, and a sophisticated metal one if your entryway leads into a modern-styled home.

A decorative touch is to use the entryway as your own art gallery. Hang several paintings, drawings or old-style family portraits on the walls. And if you can obtain it, place sculpture against one wall.

Turn a bedroom alcove or a section of a wall into valuable storage space and gain a beauty bar-vanity in the process. The vanity is just at the right height for last-minute dabbing, and the lighting is generous.

But the unit isn't only for vanity; there's plenty of storage space below the vanity, in the two closets on either side, and above the lower unit. Bed linens, nightgowns, and hand and bath towels can be stored for easy reach.

This ceiling-high unit is 6½ feet wide and 2 feet deep, wide enough for most bedrooms, and deep enough to house most beauty-bar and closet equipment. Stock materials were used throughout to minimize costs.

Set off behind the refrigerator, this alcove serves as the housewife's office by day, and an area for a child's study by night. By being between the kitchen and dining area, it helps to define each area by setting them off from each other.

Pegboard on the back of the refrigerator will take basket ornaments or letter baskets. And the facing board can be used for menus or homework and examination schedules.

By night the overhead light provides all the illumination necessary. By day, the draperies pull apart to admit daylight from the windows.

This is a convenient use of an alcove that was manufactured. The refrigerator was moved into the room to create the space.

Colored glass at the window can shut out an unwanted view, yet admit needed daylight. First, pick up several scraps of colored glass from the local glass dealer. Then cut the scraps into pieces and work them into a pattern; lay this on a sheet of clear crystal that fits your window. Glue the scraps to the crystal with silicate of soda. Fill the spaces with mastic and install the whole unit in the window opening. The pattern of the glass should be on the inside.

How to turn an alcove into a home office

Almost any small alcove can be turned into a home office. All you need are a desk, a chair, a desk light, and a few shelves for books. Once you have these basics, you can outfit an office for any member of the family.

A small alcove in the kitchen can serve as the housewife's office. In this she can place her weekly menu chart, her cookbooks, her appointment book, and her shopping list.

An under-the-stair alcove will often do duty for the man of the house providing the stairway is not used too often. When outfitting a man's office, make sure the furniture is sturdy and that there is plenty of space for office books, his favorite magazines, and even a shelf for travel folders. Check, too, that there is plenty of light. If the desk lamp is insufficient to serve the special function of his office, make certain there is an overhead lamp close by and a socket for an additional high-intensity lamp within reach.

This last provision holds true for any child's office. Young people need dashing colors to sustain their interest over a period of study time. Try not to put these offices into areas that are too small, but find space where the room allows the student to stretch out, with plenty of headroom and leg room. These may not seem important points to an adult, but they are most important considerations to a growing youngster. For this reason, make sure the desk-well provides more than ample space for the young student's legs. Within a couple of years, the space will be just right.

Doubling as a guest bedroom by night and as a rest area by day, this slant-ceiling alcove is a welcome addition to any home or apartment. The color scheme is bold and distinctive, and sets off the alcove from the rest of the room. Yet the deep green carpet belongs to the same color family as the blue spread and thus the two rooms are color coordinated.

A wall light spotlights a picture and focuses on the bed. It is the only one needed, for the alcove is bathed in a soft, light color overhead.

A small hall, one that's not easy to decorate, was given a new look with striped wallpaper. The effect was striking, but something about it proved jarring. The stripes make the room look tall but narrow. Something of the jailhouse seemed to surround a visitor within its barred walls. The color appeared to be right. The traditional desk, tastefully accessorized, looked neat. Sconces flanked a wide-matted picture, which took its color cue from the wood tones in the desk. The cheery color of the carpeting warmed the room and provided all the color that was needed. The solution to counteract the closed-in sensation did not require a color change, but what to do?

How to decorate your alcoves

Use your alcove to advantage. Let it help, not hinder, your decorating scheme. When decorating your alcove you should take all the basic facts of decorating into consideration. Once you have these firmly in your mind, you can make that little niche a charming addition to your home.

How to decorate a window dormer is often a problem. This kind of alcove does not always fit into the decorating scheme—if the decorator has overlooked what the alcove can do.

First, decide what you want to do with your dormer. Is it going to serve as a vanity or dressing table? Or a love seat? Or an office? When this has been determined, ask yourself whether you want the alcove to complement or contrast with your basic decorating scheme. Then set about to do the work.

If, for instance, the walls of the room are light and you want your dormer to contrast, paint it in a dark color. Just make sure the colors belong to the same color family. The alcove will stand out and will help your basic decorating scheme.

When the alcove has no window it has a special need for lighting. This need not be an obvious light. You can provide strip or concealed lighting to suit the purpose of the alcove. Or you can highlight the alcove with

Now compare the two rooms. Do you see what is different? A break in the stripe is exactly what was needed. A stripe, not of a different color but of a different width, brings the ceiling down and widens the room perceptibly. The choice of the wider stripe in the same color produced proportions that are more acceptable to the eye. Instead of the wall seeming to reach up to infinity, the decorative edge carries the eye around the room, not just up and down. Just one detail and the room retains its striking characteristics and stretches out as well as up. The total effect is a balanced hallway that is attractive to look at.

An old desk appears to be built-in here, and snugly fitted in an alcove. This one takes advantage of space under a stairway, space which might have been overlooked. To create a feeling of age, a piece of new aluminum grill replaces a damaged door panel below the desk top, then the scarred desk was covered with adhesive-backed paper and the corner given a uniform color appearance by the application of an antique glaze. This mood is sustained by the shelves above the desk and the wood-framed pictures facing the desk.

This storage wall takes only two feet of outward space from the room, but it is a boon in encouraging organization. Lighting is supplied under the soffit. There's a bonus not shown: part of the unit under the counter opens out to reveal a second countertop, long enough to use as a table on which to cut fabric or spread out a pattern. (To obtain this how-to-build plan, refer to PP. 2121-1 in your plans reference listing.)

an antique lamp, or a chandelier. Any of these can do the job right.

Often, you will want the alcove to be separated from the general area. When this is the case—as with a large window grouping which you intend to make into an intimate conversation area—use a divider to break it up and also to coordinate the two areas. A couch, small table, or room divider will do the job. Often a subtle change in lighting is all that is required.

The head of the bed is tucked into the alcove. The wall, painted a dark color to accent the lines of the alcove, sets off the pattern of the fabric used as a coverlet, a pattern that is repeated on the wall itself. The inside of the window frame is painted to echo the alcove, and the draperies carry the pattern of the coverlet. The light, airy window softens and balances the heaviness of the alcove. And the flowers and ferns on the scales carry this feeling of lightness into the room. To help pull the various elements together, the harmonious color treatment of the walls and rug are picked up in the throw pillows on the bed.

This alcove started off as a dark, wasted area. But by applying good decorating principles and by calling on imagination, it is now a well-lighted, functional, and decorative area that fits into the total decorating scheme.

Before any accessorizing could be done, the area had to have light. This was accomplished by inserting a glass door that introduced sunlight and also coordinated the alcove with the open-air passageway. Next, the triangle had to be removed. The answer lay in fitting in a chunky stone lion. This broke up the severe geometric line and later was used to coordinate the color scheme.

Now that the area was well lighted, there was no limit to the type or kind of accessory that could be used. In this case, candlelabras, pictures, wall lights, and a stone bowl were used. Each was balanced in relation to the sideboard.

And a plant similar to one in the passageway behind the glass door helps to draw the two areas together. Every item in the scheme has been used to fulfill a purpose.

The total color scheme, too, was not neglected when the alcove was changed. The tile floor was allowed to carry through to the wall. This helps to define the area. And the basic color, red, is picked up by the stone lion at the foot of the stair-alcove. This can also be seen in the stair carpeting, the candles, the chair seats, and the flowers.

How To Work With Aluminum In And Around Your Home

Use woodworking tools

Aluminum is strong enough for many purposes, yet can be worked with woodworking tools. You must, however, specify when you buy aluminum that you plan to work on it with hand tools. The soft alloy can be handled easily, but hundreds of aluminum alloys are made—only a few can be worked with a saw, plane, scissors, and a brace and bit. You should also be cautious when you machine it on power tools. As aluminum sawdust is hard, protect your eyes with a pair of safety glasses.

Aluminum is available in many shapes and sizes. It comes in sheets, rods, bars, angles, and tubes. There are screws, bolts, and rivets of aluminum which should be used since other metal fastenings are not as satisfactory for attaching aluminum.

An ordinary plane can cut soft-alloy aluminum. You get the best results by smoothing edges rapidly. Set the plane for fine cut. Clamp a sheet of metal between boards in a vise to hold firmly. You need to bear down hard to minimize the chatter.

To drill, you can get the cleanest hole with an auger bit. Use a twist drill for bars, angles, tubes, or rods. The taps and dies used to work steel can cut aluminum easily. Coarse threads bite best. You can use a 3/8-inch National Coarse and a 5/16-inch tap drill on aluminum.

Scissors cut aluminum easier than tin snips and can make more intricate curves. Make sure they are sharp lest they tear this tender metal. Mark the surface to be cut with an awl or ordinary crayon.

How to saw aluminum

A fine-toothed saw cuts aluminum best. To make a joint in a piece of tubing, cushion the tubing before you put it in a vise (rubber tile works well). Make a pattern of the tubing you want to insert, then scribe the pattern on the metal. Use a coping saw to cut out the piece. A half round file helps you make the final fit. A wooden plug driven into the end of the tube and secured by a screw holds fast.

Power saws make accurate cuts. Hold the aluminum tightly because the metal tends to slip on a miter gauge. If a sheet starts to rise, hold it down firmly with a block of wood.

Aluminum comes in a variety of shapes. These are some of them. From left to right are: edging, 3/8-inch rod, 1/8 × 3/4-inch and 1/4 × 1-inch bar, 1 × 1-inch angle, 5/8-, 1-, and 1¼-inch tube, and 36 × 36-inch sheets, plain or embossed. Rivets, screws, and bolts are also available to use with aluminum products. Use them for joining two pieces of aluminum or when you fasten aluminum to another metal.

You can sand aluminum with the disc-sander attachment on a portable drill or on a table saw, which can round corners or smooth saw-cuts just as it does on wood. You need to use a medium or fine-grit abrasive, because a coarse paper leaves the metal rough. Restore its polish by using a buffing wheel. A wire wheel also smooths cuts and can be used to provide a satin finish.

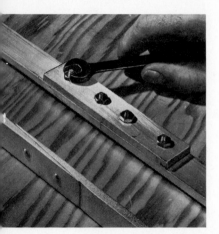

(Top left) You can join bar ends with an aluminum cleat or a long taper splice. Use aluminum rivets or bolts to secure either kind of joint. For a tight juncture, put one rivet or bolt in place first, then drill a hole for the other through both bar ends at one time. You can cut a long taper with your power saw, or you can grind it with a disc sander. Buy your aluminum bolts, rivets, or screws when you buy your stock.

To join sheet aluminum to angle or bar stock, use aluminum rivets for a joining that is tight. You can do it quickly by locking the assembly first with two or three rivets. Then you drill the two members simultaneously. A peen can help make the rivet match the metal more exactly. Use a wire wheel to remove burns left by the saw or by cutting tools. You can make rips in a bar by using the ripping fence of your saw.

(Top middle) Make a mitered corner the easy way by driving a wooden plug into the tube before you make a 45-degree angle cut. To make the cut, use a simple miter box or a table saw. The stock should be held in place firmly. A strong joint can be made by using a screw combined with glue. You may not need a screw for light work; usually just glue is enough. If you use a hardwood for the plug, pre-drill for the screw hole.

You can use doweling for several operations. Insert a piece into short tubing when you sand or buff. It makes it much easier to handle. It also helps you make a rolled edge. You make a slot in the dowel and slip the edge of the sheet into the slot. Twist the dowel while holding the roll tightly in place. To get the right size of edge, use a piece of doweling that is slightly smaller than the size of the desired roll.

(Top right) You can make a corner in angle stock by either of two ways. To make an overlapping corner, lock the angle in a vise and cut one side of it so that it is square. Do both pieces for the corner the same way. One half of each piece then overlaps the other as the right-angle bend fits together. Make the joint secure by fastening with a rivet.

If you prefer a mitered corner, make a 90-degree V-cut in the angle stock. When the stock is bent, a mitered corner is formed. Use a piece of wood to hold the angle stock firm while you are making the cut. Hand bending works well.

To make a bend in a piece of tubing, make a jig slightly smaller than the desired bend to allow for spring back. Bend the tubing around the jig by hand. For large curves you need a regular tube bender. Pack tube with wet sand to prevent crushing.

When you want to join tubes together, cut a short piece of scrap and saw a ¼-inch-wide slit in it. Use this piece as a sleeve. Slip it inside the two tubes, and it springs back to hold the pieces together. For permanent joints, use a self-tapping screw. Friction alone holds a slip joint. If the joint ends are cut true, the joint is hardly visible. The joining can be made even more invisible by applying a satin finish to the place where the tubes are joined with a turn on a wire wheel.

Another nearly invisble joint can be made when you join a rod to a bar with the self-riveted technique. You have to file the end of the rod into a round "tenon" to fit the hole drilled into the bar. Countersinking on the back of the bar fits tightly when you burr over the rivet. File off any rough surfaces and use a buffer wheel to restore the shine.

You can make a right-angle (or a more than right-angle) bend by slipping the edge of the aluminum into the slot made in a jig. If you plane the inside surface of the jig at an angle, the bend that you make is more than 90 degrees. Return to the angle you want to make a square corner.

Join sheet aluminum to tubing by sawing a slit in the tube and inserting the sheet. Bolts can be placed through both the tube walls and the sheet. You might also double-hem the aluminum sheet and squeeze the tube up and over it.

For your own safety, remember that these techniques are meant for working with soft-alloy aluminum, not hard alloys.

How To Unify A Room Around A Striking Piece Of Art

The piece of art is the figurehead of a lady above the mantel. She welcomes visitors quite literally with open arms. The rest of the room is designed to show off her charms.

The furniture and accessories are chosen to say something about the period during which figureheads rode on the prows of our stout American sailing ships. The simple lines of the furnishings repeat shapes that were used at the time. The many-drawered chest and ladder-back chairs in the dining area also hark back to that era. The turnings on the railing and the brass candlestick (now used as a lamp base) are some of the decorations common to furniture our early settlers could and did make. The difference between this room and Early American is mainly in the use of large areas of color on floors and walls.

Ambiance is from the French word meaning total environment. In interior decorating it is used to denote the effect in a decorating scheme created by accessories.

Often, one piece of art provides a key for creating a total and cohesive decorating scheme. The mood or atmosphere of the room seems to emanate from the piece of art. The color, the feeling in the room reinforces the impact of the picture, the piece of sculpture, wall hanging, or designer-carpet chosen as the starting point.

The effect may be relatively subdued or subtle. There is little unplanned in the room to create this sense of atmosphere. Once it is achieved, however, it is probably one of the most decorative and satisfying sensations in the art of decorating.

How to plan for ambiance

You begin, of course, with the work of art. Its color influences others in the room, but they are not necessarily exactly the same colors as those in the selected piece of art. It is the art you want to stress. The colors that do the most to bring out its best points are those you should choose. For example, if you want to make something stand out, you would not paint the background the same color as that which dominates the art.

The style and the period that the art represents should also be taken into consideration. You would not get the desired atmosphere by choosing a contemporary painting and then building a French provincial room setting around it. Accessories should be selected that keep in character.

Highlighted by sunlight pouring through a skylight and a recessed spotlight, an abstract painting on an easel takes center stage in this room. However, the painting and its accompaniment of green foliage create the room's accent color, not the dominant color scheme.

Nearly everything else in the room, including the accessories, comprises an analogous color scheme. The total effect of an almost one-color room is accomplished by using the related hues of red-orange, orange, and yellow-orange in varying degrees of values and intensity.

A Decorator's Guide To American Furniture Styles

The dominant influence in the American colonies in the Seventeenth Century was English, although in certain areas the French, Dutch, Spanish or other Europeans held sway. It is not surprising, therefore, that until the American Revolution those styles of furniture and furnishings that were in the mainstream of American design followed English models. In general, the American styles were several years behind their English prototypes.

The Early Colonial Period

The study of American styles generally begins with an examination of the Pilgrim settlements of New England. The furniture found there, massive and relatively crude, consisted of chairs, chests, cupboards and tables, characteristically of oak and sometimes decorated with simple carvings. Among the more common chair styles were the Carver and the Brewster (the latter, an open-sided arm chair with two rows of turned spindles on the back, the former with one row), both probably modeled on prototypes brought over from England. The most common case piece in use was the press cupboard, a massive piece with a closed top and either drawers or cabinets below.

Around 1695 the Jacobean styles of the Pilgrim settlements began to be supplanted by new furniture forms modeled on those of the William and Mary period in England. A more Baroque style, this furniture was lighter in design, was usually made of walnut and was characteristically decorated with marquetry. It was during this period that the chest-on-chest or highboy made its appearance, and it re-mained popular for the next century. William and Mary furniture, echoing the Dutch influence that William of Orange had made felt in England, frequently featured legs turned in a trumpet shape, ball or Spanish feet, and flat curving stretchers.

From about 1720 the dominant style was that of the English Queen Anne period. It met with great popularity and lasted until mid century in America, considerably longer than it held sway in its native land. Furniture from this period was typified by a lightness of form and gracefulness of line. The cabriole leg with slipper foot came into fashion. The drop leaf table with a gracefully swinging fifth leg replaced the earlier utilitarian gateleg table. Chair backs, following the English development, were made with a vase-shaped splat and a rounded crest rail. The chest-on-chest was mounted on cabriole legs and topped by a flat or scrolled pediment; it was often carved with a fan or sunburst motif.

American Chippendale

The furniture that followed the designs that originated in Georgian England is grouped under the general heading of American Chippendale. This style, which supplanted the styles of the Queen Anne period, made its appearance in the American colonies toward mid-century; it remained in vogue until about 1785. The furniture in the highest expression of this style was made in Philadelphia, but New York, Newport and Salem were also important centers. A major development of the period was the block front furniture made in New England. The finest examples came

New England shipping merchants built magnificent homes with furnishings such as porcelains from China, wallpaper and damask from France, and furniture from England. This is the parlor of the Eagle House in Haverhill, Massachusetts, as it appeared about 1818. The woodwork shows the delicate details popular during this era. Most of the furniture is in the elegant styles adapted from Neo-Classical Hepplewhite and Sheraton designs. Sheraton influences are typified by the shield back on the chair near the desk.

◄ Wise use of color, arrangement, and background creates a harmonious setting in this Early American-style contemporary dining room spiced with a French flavor. The rugged style of the table and chairs blends well with the black wrought-iron sconces and chandelier. Rich-bodied and mellow wood tones of the beams, floor, paneling, and furniture are highlighted by the soft green background of the wall. The fireplace, outlined in smooth black stone, rounds out this room, which is dramatic in effect but distinctive and comfortable in style.

A Shaker community house about 1800 probably looked just like this. The United Society of Believers in Christ's Second Appearance, nicknamed "Shakers" because of body movements made during religious meetings, was a communal society. They avoided all display, built huge barn-like structures, and made furniture without ornamentation, fine in proportion and fitting in purpose. The straightforward lines of Shaker benches are admired still. Curved backs like those on the twin desk chairs continue to be made today.

out of the Newport, Rhode Island family workshop of John Goddard and John Townsend. Generally cut from a single piece of solid mahogany, the block front has a raised section at either side and a depressed center. Shell motifs were commonly carved into the solid wood. Chippendale chairs were characterized by intricately pierced splats and either cabriole legs with the ball and claw, which was introduced at this time, or the straight Marlborough leg.

While not of the same genre, the Windsor chair, which made its first appearance in America during the first half of the eighteenth century, reached a high level of development during this period. Whether high- or low-backed, fan-, hooped-, or comb-backed, the American Windsor chair back is always made of spindles.

The Early Federal Period

Trade relations between the American colonies and England were halted by the War for Independence. When they were resumed the Neo-Classical styles of Sheraton and Hepplewhite were in vogue. The mahogany of the Chippendale period was replaced by lighter satinwood; and inlay became the preferred decoration. Chairs, in particular, reflected this desire for lightness. Classical motifs such as medallions, urns, swags, the Greek fret and pendants of husks made their appearance; chair backs were often oval or shield shaped and the lyre design or Prince of Wales feathers were sometimes employed on the splat.

(American Styles *continues on page 195, Volume 2.*)

Mount Vernon, the home of George and Martha Washington, is one of the most famous colonial homes. This is the West Parlor of Mount Vernon, which is in Fairfax County, Virginia. It is not the best example of colonial architecture, but it is typical of the larger homes of the period. Washington inherited the house after it had been in the family 83 years. After his marriage to Martha Custis, he made improvements and enlarged it. Like most planters of the period, he was probably his own architect.

Like many of his contemporaries, Washington leaned toward heavy Palladian classic forms. The doorway illustrates this style. The rest of the room has raised paneling, which was common in older homes. The corner fireplace has been ornamented with raised leafy scrolls. Between the scrolls at the top is the coat of arms of the Washington family.

The furniture indicates that this room was decorated rather late in Washington's life. The Sheraton and Hepplewhite styles date from the Early Federal period. The upholstered chair next to the fireplace is the so-called "Martha Washington" style. On the coffee table is a Lowestoft tea set. The rug is like the French Aubusson carpets that were presented to George Washington.

About 1752 the great hall in a Pennsylvania Dutch house looked this way. The Pennsylvania Dutch were colonists from the Rhineland. Most of them were Germans and members of the Mennonite, Amish, Moravian, and Dunker sects who settled around Philadelphia and along the Delaware and Susquehanna rivers. When you travel through this country today, you can still see the great stone houses and huge red barns. Sometimes the barns have a brightly painted round disc called the "hexenfoos" device, designed to protect the barn from evil spirits. Sometimes these "hexes" were painted on furniture inside the house too.

This room is a reproduction of the Jerg Muler house, built in 1752. The mantel beam is nearly 10 feet long and made from one piece of oak. The corner staircase and the raised and carved panels on the doors are unusual and beautiful.

Elaborate cupboards, made of pine and oak, were filled with pewter, brass, and pottery. The brightly painted pottery was made in Pennsylvania, but the designs were brought from the old country. The chairs are carved, erect, and stiff. Notice the spinning wheel decorated with painted designs and the chest ornamented with folk figures.

This is a replica of the George Washington Smith house in Santa Barbara, California. It shows a contemporary use of Mission furniture. Just as the Puritans adapted the styles they knew to suit their new circumstances, so did the Western pioneers. They adapted some of their styles to suit the climate and adopted others from the Spanish colonists who settled this land.

Santa Barbara is justly proud of its Franciscan Mission, built in 1820. This home suggests, rather than copies, the styles pioneers from the East found here when they arrived. Spanish architecture suits the climate. The high ceilings and thick walls keep out summer heat. The white walls add to the feeling of coolness and make a good background for bright colors. The uncovered tile floor is also cool.

The designs here are of types found in Spain from the Fifteenth to Eighteenth Centuries. Carving is deep and ornate. The paneled chest is similar to today's Spanish styles.

Bright-colored tile trims the doorway and mounts the stairs. The geometric designs are reminiscent of Moorish elements found in Spain.

Master/Guide

Abacá

An extremely tough and durable fiber. Also known as Manila and Manila hemp, it is used primarily in woven matting, carpeting, wall covering and in making rope.

Generally, the term "hemp" (or abacá, since the terms are practically synonymous) is applied to the product of several fibers. And the outstanding characteristic of these fibers is their inherent ability to withstand water, sun and wind—better than other natural fibers.

Since its quality of resistance is so high, abacá fiber is ideal for furnishings that are destined to get hard wear or exposure to sun, water and wind. And although being replaced by newer synthetic fibers, it can still add that needed decorative touch or be durable enough for, say, that outdoor patio you're planning.

Abachi

A wood that comes from Eastern Africa, and is similar to primavera. It is often called ayous. The wood is creamy white to pale yellow in color, and shows a faint striped pattern when quartered. It is lightweight, soft, and has a consistent texture. When used commercially, the veneers have a regular figure similar to mahogany.

Abacus

In architecture, this is the topmost slab of the capital on a column, whose shape depends on the style of the column. It also appears on columns used in furniture, such as a Grandfather clock. It is also a counting device used as an accessory in Oriental decors.

Abassi Cotton

An Egyptian cotton with a silk-like sheen. It is a long staple cotton (from 1¼ to 1½ inches), quite fine and nearly white. It is manufactured into a fine cloth that can be bleached, dyed and mercerized. Fabrics made from abassi cotton take a glossy finish, even on sheer materials, yet are strong and wear well. The fiber's counterpart in the United States is a long staple cotton with a fine luster that is grown in the Southwest.

Abattant

A piece of furniture with a drop front. The

word "abattant" is from the French *abattre,* which means to lower or fall down. Shown above is a *secrétaire à abattant* or drop-leaf secretary.

ABC's of Decorating

Basic introduction to various areas of home decorating. Suggestions for handling color, accessories, etc., are briefly outlined. See *ABC's of Decorating,* p. 14.

Abnakee Rug

An American hooked rug with bold designs and coarse construction. The backing is made of jute, and the hooking material is un-bleached flannel or similar-weight wool.

Aboudikŕou

A wood from Eastern Africa used for furniture veneers. It is tough, heavier than African mahogany, red-brown in color. Pattern is usually striped. It is available in lumber or veneer for use in furniture, cabinetry or interior paneling. It is also called Sipo, Tiama or Sapele.

Abraded Filament Yarns

Continuous filament yarns whose surface has been broken by being passed over a rough surface are known as abraded. Because of their broken fibers, they cover better than continuous filament yarns and are stronger than spun yarns. They can be dyed without losing their matte finish. They are commonly twisted with other yarns, although they can be used singly if twisted properly.

Abrasion Resistance

The ability of a material to withstand wear and rubbing. Plastic table and dresser tops are abrasion and heat resistant. New varnishes resist scratches, and vinyl flooring has added years to floors because it resists scuffs and is resilient.

Many manufacturers test fabrics on a wear-test machine. It usually holds two materials at a time to compare their wearing qualities. The abradant, a flexible aloxite cloth or a piece of cloth like that being tested, and the material are rubbed against each other. The results indicate the degree to which fabrics resist surface wear. Testing programs such as this enable a manufacturer to determine which weaves and fibers are the most durable. Of course, there are other similar tests that a manufacturer may use also.

Abrasives

Substances such as sandpaper or emery cloth that are used for smoothing and polishing various materials. See *Abrasives,* p. 44.

Absorbents

Substances that gather up other substances. Acoustical tile absorbs sound because the porous materials from which it is made absorb sound waves instead of reflecting them to produce an echo. Drapes and carpeting have much the same effect.

Chemicals used for stain removal also have absorptive powers. Spread a chemical, such as one of the dry rug cleaners, over the surface, and it absorbs dirt and stains. Often cleaning products have chemicals to loosen soil as well as an absorbent material that picks up grease and dirt.

Corn meal, fuller's earth and chalk are absorbents. They are used primarily for picking up light, freshly made stains. Absorbent cotton is another product that is a household item. It absorbs because the natural waxy oils have been removed from it. This way, it can pick up and hold water or other liquids.

In other words, absorption is the taking in and holding of some material in some manner; much like, for example, a sponge takes in water and holds it in its pores, or a paper towel with its absorbent fibers that allow liquids to cling to them without their breaking apart. And this absorption and the rate of absorbency play an important part in the make-up of various fabrics.

Manufacturers of fabrics use a gauge that measures the rate of absorbency of a textile. The fabric is dipped into water and potassium bichromate. The speed with which the liquid is absorbed can then be measured. This is important because the less the absorption, the greater the stability of the fabric. This indicates that the fabric won't stretch or shrink.

Abutment

In architecture, the support below the arch, which bears the weight, withstands the down-

ward thrust. In furniture manufacture, it is the place where two woods adjoin.

Acacia
A tree similar to the locust, sometimes called mimosa, which thrives in warm countries. The wood is heavy and strong, but not commercially important. Myrtle Burl, mistakenly called Acacia Burl, is used for furniture, cabinetry and interior paneling. In Africa, acacias yield valuable gum arabic.

Acanthus
A conventionalized leafy decoration based on the leaf of a plant that grows in Asia, Africa

and southern Europe. The classic Greek and Roman design is found at the top of Corinthian columns and has been revived in many furniture styles.

Accent and Area Rugs
These smaller-than-room-size carpets are as ancient as homes. From the time of rush matting they've been used to keep feet from the cold floor. Decorative rugs, often resembling the ones shown above, were made centuries ago in China and Persia. Today they are still popular. They supply accent color and help hold a furniture grouping together. They protect wall-to-wall carpeting in a hallway or supply textural variety when hung on a wall. See *Accent and Area Rugs,* p. 96.

Accent Color
Wherever you find the accent color, that's

where the action is. Accent colors frequently are strong, but they need not always pack a wallop. Accent colors can be calming neutrals as well as brilliant hues.

Accent colors are not limited to use in little accessories. They may appear anywhere—a whole wall, around or in the glass at the window, in fabrics on furniture, or on the floor. They are the third or fourth color in a scheme. In the picture below, red accents brighten the blue, the green and the neutral in this room. See *ABC's of Decorating, Color,* pps. 18-23; and *Color.*

Accessories and Accents
The things you add to support items of

greater importance. They are the symbols of your taste, designs you find pleasing or amusing. They produce individuality since no two people choose exactly the same things. They can be gay or sober, but should always be expressive of you and your living.

Not all accessories are purely decorative. Some, such as clocks, lamps, books and ashtrays are purposeful; but they work just as well if they're decorative, suit the style of the room, the space they occupy and the color scheme in the room.

When looking for a center of interest, you can always depend on accessories to create one for you. A wall filled with shelves attracts the eye. One picture or a group of them, an area rug or a display of things you collect are accessories that sometimes are strong enough to command all the attention you need.

While there are not a lot of rules regarding the use of accessories, there are some suggestions that can help you produce a less clut-

Accessories (cont.)

tered, more organized approach to handling your accessories. (As a matter of fact, here's where you can use imagination and be daring.) These hints center around the artistic rules for creating harmony, not only in color, but in proportion and style.

There's certainly no mystique about using accessories, but there are ways that you can train your eye to see relationships.

Accessories can create height, carry the eye around the room, or draw attention to an object or area—just where you want it. They can dress up a table, or calm down a couch with neutral pillows. See *Accessories and Accents,* p. 46; *Ambiance,* p. 174.

Accordion Pleats

A series of folds that resemble those in the bellows of an accordion. These folds vary from ⅛- to ½-inch in size. They're seen on box spring covers, chair drops, and draperies.

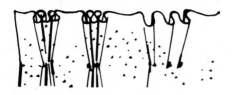

Acetate

A fiber, yarn, thread or fabric developed from cellulose, produced by the acetate process of manufacture. It isn't a regenerated cellulose (which is made from wood pulp) like viscose rayon, but is an ester of cellulose, hence the name, cellulose acetate. While acetate fabrics hang well and take dye well, they do have limitations as to their use.

Because they start from the same base, cellulose acetate might be expected to have similar characteristics to rayon. Actually, while they do share some similarities, the two fibers differ enough to warrant a ruling by the Federal Trade Commission. In 1952, the F.T.C. decided that the term "rayon" applied to man-made textile fibers and filaments composed of regenerated cellulose and the yarn, thread, or fabrics made from these fibers and filaments. "Acetate" applied to man-made textiles, fibers and filaments composed of cellulose acetate and the yarn, thread and fabric made of such fibers and filaments.

Acetate has other physical and chemical properties than does rayon. Its reaction to dyes is so different that a set of dyes had to be developed. When a high proportion (92 percent) of the fibers are acetylated, the term "triacetate" may be used as a generic description of the fiber.

Acetate is used in curtains, carpets, and in blended fabrics. Dry cleaning is recommended, since acetone and alcohol dissolve acetate fibers. Acetate fabrics have been made stronger by new manufacturing processes and by combining acetate with other fibers.

Achromatic

Literally, without color. When applied to color it specifies the neutral tones: blacks, grays and whites. See *ABC's of Decorating, Color,* p. 18-23; and *Color.*

Acorn

A type of turning that resembles the shape of an acorn. It is particularly popular in Jacobean styles on chair and bed posts and pendants.

Acoustics

The science of sound and its influence on people. In home furnishings, porous materials such as acoustical tile, soft-textured rugs, draperies, and upholstered furniture absorb sound. One of the more interesting sound-absorbing materials for walls is carpeting that covers the four walls. A similar effect is obtained with acoustical tile.

In architecture, acoustics deals with making buildings quieter or providing ideal conditions for listening to music or speech.

It's a branch of physics but uses psychology to test its influence on people.

Acrilan

The registered trademark of The Chemstrand Corporation for its acrylic fiber. It is made up of a long chain of synthetic polymer composed of at least 85 percent by weight acrylonitrile—a liquid derived from natural gas and air. Acrilan and Acrilan 16, which have slightly different chemical properties, may be combined to produce cross-dyed effects. Both products are available in staple fiber form or as continuous filament flow.

Acrilan can be combined with other man-made fibers or with wool, or used as the only material in a fabric. It can be spun on the same machines that spin cotton and wool. The resultant fabric is characterized by a marked resemblance to wool. It is warm and lightweight and highly resistant to wrinkling and chemical or bacterial attacks. Fabrics made from Acrilan can be machine washed with detergents, then machine dried. They resist mildew and moth damage. Acrilan is used for floor coverings, clothes, blankets, draperies, and upholstery fabrics. Industrially, it is used in many places where chemically resistant fabrics are most needed.

The Chemstrand Corporation owns the trademark and licenses its use to other companies.

Acroterium

An ornament or statue erected on the gable or roof corners of a building. Used originally on Greek temples, similar ornaments are used on the top corners of secretaries, highboys and other large furniture.

Acrylic

Designates acrylic acid and substances made from it. Acrylic acid is colorless, has a sharp odor. It is soluble in water and alcohol and is used in the manufacture of various plastics and fibers. True acrylics include Acrilan (composed of 85 percent acrylonitrile), Creslan, "Orlon" and Zefran. Dynel and Verel are made from modified acrylic fibers and therefore are classified as Modacrylic fibers.

Acrylic Resins

A group of thermoplastic resins made synthetically from the polymerization of the esters of acrylic acid or one of its derivatives. Thermoplastic materials can be melted and they harden again when cooled. Polymers are chain-like structures from which synthetic fibers are made.

Acrylic resins are tough plastics, crystal clear and highly resistant to sunlight and water as well as acids, alcohol, alkalies, mineral oils and water.

These plastics are easily colored, have high impact strength. Consequently they can be used for accessories such as tail lights, shoe heels, and optical lenses.

Adam, Robert (1728-1792)

The most famous of four brothers, all architects and sons of a Scottish architect, Robert is renowned for the creation of an architectural and furniture style that flourished in the last half of the Eighteenth Century. His portrait appears above. (The original hangs in the National Portrait Gallery in London.) His designs, characterized by their delicacy and refinement, reflect his interest in classical styles, particularly Roman ones, and his efforts to keep the best of ancient cultures alive.

The creation of the Adam Style came largely as a result of his travels. In Italy, his companion was Charles Louis Clérisseau, a French architect and antiquary. He also met Giovanni Battista Piranesi, an etcher, architect and archeologist whose opinions he admired. Adam's early sketches show the influences of these associations.

Robert Adam with Clérisseau went to Spalato, in Dalmatia, where he sketched Roman ruins. He later published these sketches in a book entitled *The Ruins of the Palace of the Emperor Diocletian*. He studied the archeology of Italy, Greece, Syria and Dalmatia, thus gaining knowledge of ancient designs. He was fascinated by the excavations at Herculaneum, and was influenced by Roman interior design and the works of Michelangelo, Raphael and Domenichino.

Adam returned to England and began his career as an architect in 1759. His brother James (1730-1794) joined him in 1761, and in 1773 they published their first volume of *The Works of Robert and James Adam*. Much of their philosophy of decoration, which dominated English designs for half a century, is contained in these *Works*. The Adam brothers believed that every detail of a house and its furnishings should come from one mind.

The silver cup, below, is an example of Adam Style. Notice its classic shape, exquisitely fine details which are painstakingly executed. Plant forms festoon the handle.

Adam furniture was designed to accompany architectural designs. The wooden cabinet,

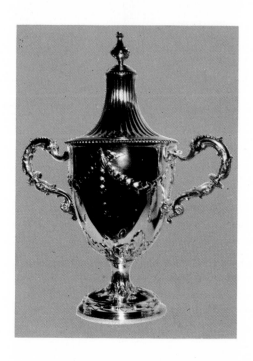

above, shows typical decoration used in the Adam style. The cabinet is ornamented with marquetry (figurative inlays of contrasting woods), painting and gilt bronze. Recurring motifs that enrich the surfaces are drapery swags, medallions, vases and urns, lyres and arabesques. The arabesques are the leafy scroll work you see in bands around the top and bottom of the cabinet. Arabesques on the furniture relate to those on the wall panels, typical of Adam interiors where even tiny accessories match.

The Adam brothers hired cabinetmakers, painters and sculptors to execute their designs. Among them were Hepplewhite, Angelica Kauffmann and other famous craftsmen.

Adam Architecture

Robert Adam's first important commission after his return to England in 1759 was the erection of the columnar screen in front of the Admiralty, Whitehall, London. Two years later he served with Sir William Chambers as Architect of His Majesty's Works.

When his brother James joined him he was already receiving many commissions for the redecoration or extension of country homes. In 1762 he redesigned the interior of Syon House in Middlesex in Neo-Classic Style.

Designers, like Adam, who use classical lines, are said to belong to the Palladian School of Architecture—which derives its name from Andrea Palladio (1518-1580). This native Italian had an elegant style; he standardized classical architecture and designed what became known as the Palladian arch. This is now any arched opening supported on columns flanked by narrow openings the same height as the columns.

In Syon House, Adam used a variety of contrasting geometrical shapes inspired by classical prototypes. In the Jacobean Long Gallery, a great amount of detailed decoration is applied around twelve Ionic columns. The space above and between the columns has detached statues. Adam designed a Pantheon, a replica of the Athenian temple, for the central court, but it was never built. The idea, however, was used

The greatest joint work of James and Robert was the Adelphi in London. It was built in 1768 and was at the time a huge undertaking. Several streets of houses were planned, a forerunner of our planned communities or neighborhoods.

Adam worked mostly in London between 1762 and 1774. During that time he designed the magnificent library for Kenwood, Hempstead. The sketch for this room is shown below. In it you can see the many classical elements Adam used. Corinthian columns with their traditional crown of acanthus leaves flank arched niches next to the fireplace. Stylized decorative motifs are lavishly applied. Notice the twin settees tucked into the niches

and how they are secondary to the wealth of architectural detail.

Adam furniture and accessories are always adjuncts to architectural designs. In their books, Robert and James express their philosophy of the unity of architecture, furniture and accessories. When they designed a building, they designed all that went into it. This unity was new to English architecture, and came from France where the approach was used in palaces.

The distinguishing features of Adam Style are a preference for straight lines or square silhouettes. Adam used swags, festoons, and continuous spiral or wavy ornaments called rinceaux (called branching scroll when intertwined with stems and leaves). All these decorations are free in form. Mythological figures such as rams' heads, lions' heads and claws, centaurs, and griffins mingle with plant forms and Greek and Roman vases. These details are executed in paint, low-relief carving, inlay and composition, a mixture of whiting, resin and size, which is molded into carved shapes

and applied to the furniture, forming raised designs.

The Adam brothers helped change the popularity of certain furniture woods. For their early furniture they used mahogany, but later helped initiate the Age of Satinwood. Later came harewood (sycamore dyed gray). Sometimes whole pieces of furniture were painted white or green, then gilded and painted with delicate designs. Many experts point out the similarities between Adam and Louis XVI Styles. Others maintain that his designs were a result of revived interest in Roman styles.

The room shown below is based on the entrance hall of No. 1 Bedford Square in London. It shows the Adam Style as interpreted by contemporaries. The furniture is Adam-Hepplewhite. The cameo plaques on the sconces are Wedgwood. The furniture is secondary in importance to the room setting.

Adam Style has great charm and refinement, but its perfection produced the criticism that it was excessively polite, lacking in warmth and livability.

Adapting Color Schemes

When continuing colors from one room to another, individual rooms do not necessarily have to be done to the same proportion. The dining room, at right, is decorated in shades of blue, green and white. The inspiration for this color scheme was taken from the adjoining living room. The living room colors have been "adapted" to the dining room. Less blue and less green were used in this room, but the two rooms harmonize with one another. This kind of harmony promotes a look of total home decorating.

A color scheme that you see in a friend's house or in a magazine may be appealing to you. If so, "adapt" the colors you see and like to a room in your home. To make this transposition you need to study the colors used. Try to find the key to the color—the note that sets the theme. You can make a list of colors to help you remember them and the furnishings in which they appear. Notice the proportions in which each color is used. Then adapt the scheme by using the same colors in similar proportions to fit your own room. See *Color*.

Adaptations

Styles from the past that have been changed to suit modern living. Classical styles, those that have proven popular over the years, are rescaled for modern rooms. New furniture construction techniques, upholstery materials for filling, and coverings and protective finishes make changes necessary. As you can see in the three pictures on these pages, the chairs have the flavor of the original designs, but they incorporate all the latest in materials, too.

The chair, at left, is in Adam Style, designed during the third quarter of the Eighteenth Century. It shows the delicate detail characteristic of Adam and the softening of lines, which seems to show an influence of the French Louis XVI Style. The chair at upper right is a contemporary version of a French country piece. The armchair at lower right is a modern cousin of larger overstuffed pieces, now scaled down.

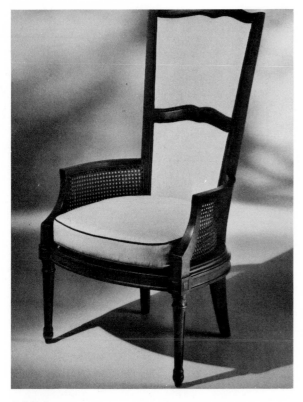

Additions

A room or rooms built onto a home. A family's need for space changes as the years pass. If you like your present house and location, your best bet in dollars and convenience may be to build an addition. See *Additions,* p. 110.

Adequate Wiring

Sufficient electrical wiring and power to handle today's increased demands for electricity. See *Adequate Wiring,* p. 118.

Adobe

Spanish word for dried brick. The word *adobe* is used for the clay block as well as the sun-dried brick. The brick is used as a building material in the southwestern United States, particularly in California, Arizona and New Mexico. It has an appealing texture and is a good insulator against the hot summer sun.

Affleck, Thomas (?-1795)

Scottish-born American cabinet maker brought to Philadelphia by John Penn in 1763. He was influenced by Chippendale patterns, and produced furniture with square Marlborough legs.

Afghan

A knitted or crocheted blanket made of woolen or synthetic yarns. It may be used as a throw or color accent on a sofa, the foot of a bed, or wherever you need it. Some museum examples date back several centuries.

Agate, Agate Ware and Agate Glass

Agate is a fine-grained variety of quartz, streaked with many colors. Onyx agate and bull's-eye agate have marble-like markings. Moss agate contains delicate fern patterns.

Agate ware was produced commercially in Staffordshire, England, about 1750. Earthenware and stoneware resembling agate were made by mixing different colored clays or combining different slips. Josiah Wedgwood refined the process to resemble semiprecious stones.

Agate glass, made by melting different colors of glass together, resembles mineral agate. It was popular during the Renaissance and later in England and America as decorations.

Agglomerate

An extrusive rock, formed by volcanic action when magma is forced out onto the surface of the earth. Pieces of rock are cemented together by a natural cement. Also called volcanic breccias, it is used in building.

Aggregates

Materials such as sand, gravel, crushed rock or blast furnace slag which, when combined with cement and water, form concrete. See *Paved Areas*.

Air Conditioning

The cooling and dehumidifying of rooms by mechanical means. Two types are widely used, room-sized and central air conditioners. See *Air Conditioning,* p. 158.

Alabaster

Most common type is a marble-like material, used frequently in ornaments; it is a special type of gypsum made of hydrated sulphate of lime. It has a fine grain, is white or delicately tinted in color and extremely soft. A harder kind of alabaster, made of carbonate of lime such as that found in stalactites and stalagmites, is harder than gypsum.

Alcoves

Small, recessed places in a building. They have decorative and functional uses. Created alcoves can provide storage space. See *Alcoves,* p. 162.

Alkyd paints

Used as primer and primer-sealers, they are made from alkyd resin dissolved in mineral spirits. They dry overnight, are suitable for all interior surfaces except unprimed dry-wall and those containing active alkali such as damp plaster or masonry. As finish coats, they are practically impervious to water; they dry relatively fast; they resist abrasion and impact. They are also a replacement for oil paints.

Almond

As a decoration, an oval-shaped pendant of cut glass or crystal that hangs on a chandelier, so named because it resembles the shape of an almond nut. Also, the hardwood tree that grows near the Mediterranean and bears nuts.

Alloys

Mixtures of two or more metals made to produce certain characteristics. They are generally harder and less malleable than the metals from which they are made. Brass, bronze, pewter and stainless steel are alloys.

Alpaca

An animal, native to the Andes mountains, whose fleece is made into a fine fabric. Alpaca fabric is soft, lightweight, with a silken sheen that resembles mohair.

Aluminum

A lightweight, silvery blue metal that resists oxidation and tarnishing. It is often used for furniture frames and outdoor furniture. Soft alloys can be worked with woodworking tools. See *Aluminum,* p. 171.

Ambiance

The arrangement of accessories to intensify the effect of a piece of decorative art. Color promotes the effect. See *Ambiance,* p. 173.

Amboyna

A burl-patterned hardwood grown in the East Indies which was popular with Adam and Hepplewhite as a furniture veneer in the Eighteenth Century.

American Styles

The styles and designs that flourished in our country. They reflect the country's progress and technology. See *American Styles,* p. 175.